FURTHER STEPS
IN FAMILY HISTORY

FURTHER STEPS
IN FAMILY HISTORY

GUIDED BY EVE McLAUGHLIN

COUNTRYSIDE BOOKS
NEWBURY, BERKSHIRE

Other Genealogical Titles available from Countryside Books include:

FIRST STEPS IN FAMILY HISTORY
Eve McLaughlin

BEGINNING YOUR FAMILY HISTORY
George Pelling

SHORT CUTS IN FAMILY HISTORY
Michael Gandy

LOOKING AT OLD PHOTOGRAPHS
Robert Pols

TRACING YOUR FAMILY TREE
Jean Cole & John Titford

08261787

First Published 1990
© Eve McLaughlin 1990
Revised and Updated 1999

COUNTRYSIDE BOOKS
3 Catherine Road
Newbury, Berkshire

ISBN 1 85306 602 8

*Based on the individual booklets published as part of the
McLaughlin Guide Series*

Produced through MRM Associates Ltd., Reading
Typeset by Acorn Bookwork, Salisbury
Printed by Woolnough Bookbinding, Irthlingborough

CONTENTS

The BLOGGS FAMILY in Sprotley, Loamshire

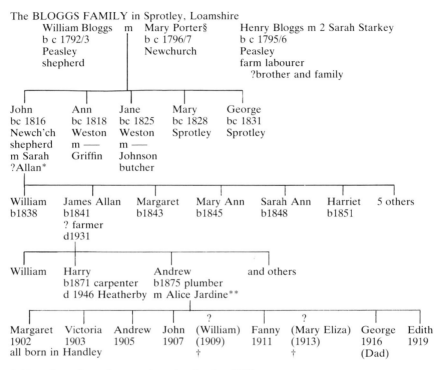

§ Mary Porter's mother was Ann, her brother William, a carter.
* Sarah Allan was the daughter of James Allan b c1770 in Auchterarder, Perth, Scotland, a gardener, presumably to the Hon. Mr Dennison. Her? brothers, Andrew and Robert, were also his gardeners.
** sister of Bartholomew Jardine b 1880 Newcastle. Innkeeper in Handley d 1937.
† same registration district as known children, born + died in those years

6

INTRODUCTION

Starting on the trail of your ancestors is like climbing down a mountain in the dusk – once you have started, it is hard to stop, but easy to go astray and waste time and energy. There are different paths which may reach the same objective, but some take longer than they should and others are dead ends from which you must retrace your steps. If you know what markers to look out for, and follow every lead, you will get there, and the results are pretty exhilarating.

Some of you will already have *First Steps in Family History*, in which I took an imaginary family named Bloggs and showed how they (or indeed any other family like them) could be traced back from the 1940s to the early years of the nineteenth century, using mainly certificates of birth, marriage and death, censuses and modern wills. The information gained will enable you to draw up a family tree similar to that I have made for the Bloggs family, opposite.

But how do you begin to track down ancestors before National Registration began in 1837? This book aims to guide you in your quest back as far as Tudor times and beyond. It will equip you with the vital techniques and information needed to find your way through highways and byways of document research to a satisfyingly full family history.

I wish you a good deal of enjoyment along the way.

Eve McLaughlin

BAPTISMS folemnized in the Parifh of _Handborough._
in the County of _Oxon_ in the Year 18**27**

| When Baptized. | Child's Chriftian Name. | Parents Name. | | Abode. | Quality, Trade, or Profeffion. | By whom the Ceremony was performed. |
		Chriftian.	Surname.			
1827. June 3 No. 425.	June 3 Susan daughter of	Susan	William and Elizabeth	Buckingham — Handbro.	Labourer	Thos Spindle Curate
June 3? No. 426.	Amelia daughter of	James & Mary	Long	Handbro	Tradesman	Thos Spindle Curate
July 15th No. 427.	Anne Mary illegitimate daughter of	Dinah	Leach	Handbro.		Thos Spindle Curate

Nineteenth century registers
*Entries of Baptisms and Burials at Han(d)borough, Oxfordshire, in the
standard printed form books introduced by Rose's Act from 1837. Note
the curate has got the columns muddled in the first entry.*

BURIALS in the Parifh of _Handborough_
in the County of _Oxford_ in the Year 18**47**

Name.	Abode.	When buried.	Age.	By whom the Ceremony was performed.
Sarah Slatter No. 649.	Long Handbro'	July 2	49	J. Robinson
Rosetta Woodward No. 650.	Witney, Union Workhouse	July 20	5 mths	Frank B. Wright Curate

8

PARISH REGISTERS

The events you now seek happened before July 1837, when national registration began (or even after that date and the birth was not registered). The first course is usually to consult parish registers.

Why are they not a perfect alternative (and cheaper) source after 1837? They may be useful, but only if your family continued to worship in the Church of England. Parish church attendance tailed off in the last century, in towns more rapidly than in the country, as suburban churches were built and other denominations competed. Many families went to some kind of non-conformist chapel for a period and eventually, the bulk of the population ceased to attend any form of church regularly. Marriages continued to take place mainly in church, though a register office wedding was possible from 1837, and chapels steadily became licensed to hold marriages as well. Only in recent times have the clergy objected to having their churches used as an attractive accessory to wedding photos, by people who never darken their doors at other times.

However, it is from the middle of the 19th century and back that parish registers become a primary source of information. Census entries will show a birthplace, and an age (which may be approximate). The next stage is to discover if the events are catalogued in the registers of that parish.

Assuming that your family were good Church of England folk, and stayed in one place, will the registers give you all you need? Possibly not, since the amount of detail is not the same as in certificates.

Marriage registers after 1st July 1837 do give exactly the same information. There are two entries to a page, identical in form with certificates. They will tell you the *names of groom and bride*; the *ages*, exact or 'full', meaning 21 or more; the *marital status; the occupation*, of the groom at least; the *place of residence*, which may be just 'of this parish'; the *name and occupation of the two fathers*. You also get the actual signatures (or marks) of the couple and their witnesses. However, you cannot usually photocopy the entries for less than £5.50, as decreed by the Registrar General. Most Record Offices will permit a photograph, however and a few will photocopy.

The snag is that marriages do not necessarily take place where the couple later lived. It was common to marry in the bride's home parish, or where she was working at the time. You could search for years for a Hampshire couple who happened to marry in London or Gloucester. National registration gets over this problem with a consolidated index for the whole of England and Wales from 1837 (with a similar Scottish index from 1855 and an Irish (Protestant) one from 1845).

Baptism and burial registers show less detail than the equivalent certificates of birth and death. You can judge if this matters.

Baptismal entries probably will not show the date of birth, and baptism may be much delayed. They also very rarely indeed show the maiden name of the mother. You may have it from other sources, but things can get confusing if there are two John and Mary Smiths, or if one man marries two wives of the same name in succession. Carefully cross-checking with burial registers and censuses is necessary.

However, some births in the earlier years of registration (and even later in cities) were never officially notified, so that the census and baptismal entries are the only evidence of existence. Parish register entries are accepted as proof of age for pensions purposes therefore, and parents who left it late lose their offspring money. The unbaptised have to rely on tracing midwives in their nineties, or finding certain other documentary evidence.

Burial registers do not give the precise date of death, the marital status, occupation, cause of death, or the name of the informant (a probable relative). They do give *ages* – not necessarily accurate, nor the same as the certificate age. As a bonus, they may state the normal address or parish of someone who happens to die while visiting a daughter – which a certificate in England would not. If the death was violent or sudden, the register should note 'by coroner's order' which will alert you to look for an inquest report in the local paper.

Unless you come from a family of zealous churchgoers, the value of parish registers to you will diminish as the century wears on. Searching a city parish, or several of them, is a very time-consuming business. A combination of certificates and censuses can take you more rapidly back to 1837, and it is before this that the parish registers may become your prime source.

Parish registers from 1813

Rose's Act of 1812 established for the first time a printed format for baptism and burial registers and amended marriage registers slightly. The *baptismal registers* provided columns for the *date of baptism*, the *surname* and *Christian name of the child and its parents*, the *occupation of the father* and their *residence*. In the country this was probably just the village or hamlet name, or possibly a farm, though in towns a street address is normally given. The final column gives the signature of the clergyman. Sometimes, conscientious clergy squeeze a date of birth into the margin. There are eight entries to a page.

In the case of illegitimate children, the mother's Christian and surname is stated (and, occasionally, the father's full name too) with the addition of 'base born' and her occupation, or 'spinster', 'single', in the penultimate column. Alternatively, the child may be given the father's full name as forenames, 'John Smith Jones, base-born of Mary Jones', with the hope that they would later marry and the second surname could be dropped. Double forenames were then rare, except in the gentry and upper middle classes, outside London and Yorkshire.

Burial registers have similar columns, with space for the *date*, *Christian* and *surname*, *age* and *residence* of the deceased, but not, unfortunately, the occupation or any other comment, which had sometimes been added to burial entries in plain-paged registers. Just occasionally, nevertheless, remarks are added – regularly if the burial is 'by coroner's warrant', possibly if the death was in odd circumstances or that of a gentleman, cleric or parish clerk. The 'name of officiating clergyman' is rarely important, though worth noting if it is not the usual one – he may be a relative.

This type of baptism and burial register continued after 1837, until modern times. The marriage registers, however, changed completely in 1837, to the 'certificate' form.

There had been printed *marriage registers* since 1754, and Rose's Act merely changed the number of entries per page from four to three. There were blank spaces on the pages in which the clerk or clergyman had to write the *names* and *parishes* of the parties, and the *date*. There was room to include the *marital status* of both, but this is sometimes omitted. There was a space to show if the marriage was by *licence* or *banns*, and, if one or both was *under 21*, a '*minor*', then room to write 'with consent of father/parents'. Some clergy got confused and entered 'with consent of friends' for the marriages of adults who needed no such agreement. The couple then had to sign, or make a mark to their names. Occasionally, the signature does not tally completely with the spelling of the name written above. The clergyman himself then signed, and two or more *witnesses*. These tended to be relatives (contemporaries rather than parents), though lonely folk might call in people who lived near the church. Look out for a very regular signature, which may be that of the parish clerk.

Before 1837, everyone (except Jews and Quakers) had to be married in church, even if they were strict Baptists or 'Independents'. From July 1837, chapel members could wed in their own chapel, if it was licensed for the purpose, which may not have happened till 1890. Civil marriage before the Registrar was possible from July 1837, though many continued to use the parish church for weddings only. By 1900, about ten per cent of couples were married in a Registry Office.

Marriage Registers from 1754: the Hardwicke Act

In theory, marriages were always supposed to have taken place in the parish church, if by banns, though those who could afford licences could marry elsewhere, normally in a nominated church. However, there was nothing to prevent any person who had ever taken Holy Orders, whether or not he was a beneficed clergyman, from marrying anyone anywhere at any time. By the middle of the 18th century, this had led to great abuses, and various runaway marriages of heiresses had made this a problem to the legislating classes. Philip Yorke, Lord Hardwicke, therefore introduced in 1753 the Act which bears his name, whose purpose was 'the better prevention of clandestine marriages'.

From March 1754, marriages were only legal if they took place after banns in the parish church of one of the parties, often that of the bride, normally by the parish clergyman, though he could permit another beneficed clergyman, such as a relative of the parties, to officiate. Alternatively, marriages by licence were still permitted at churches where banns had formerly been accustomed to be published, which cut the old 'marriage shops'. New churches built to cope with increased population in some areas had to be specifically licensed before legal marriages could take place.

Registers in compliance with the Act are generally about 18″ tall, often covered in brown suede, and each page contains four printed forms with spaces to insert the variable details. The *name* of bride and groom, the *parish* of both and quite frequently the *marital status* and sometimes the man's *occupation* could be entered, also the *date* of the ceremony, and whether it was by *banns* or *licence*. The *signatures* of the couple, the clergyman and two or more *witnesses* were also demanded, for the first time. If they could not write, they made marks to their names written by the clerk.

Because the number of entries per page was standard, it was no longer possible to forge an extra one or cut out an entry without its showing. Even when this was done, the entry could be traced in the copy sent to the bishop each year. Most of the clergy numbered each entry as well, for even greater security. The witnesses who signed could be called to vouch for the accuracy of the record too.

It should be borne in mind that 'of this parish' does not necessarily imply long residence there. Three weeks was the legal requirement, though the more conscientious clergy would describe such an incomer as 'sojourner here', and, rarely, even note his actual parish of settlement. Sometimes the motive for moving into a parish before the marriage was to avoid two sets of banns fees, and the trouble of collecting a certificate (that they had been called) from the distant parish.

The main purpose of the Act had been to prevent runaway marriages of heiresses and consequent loss of control of their fortunes. Minors needed the consent of their parent to contract a valid marriage anyway and even with slightly older heiresses, parish clergy were vulnerable to pressure if they allowed such a marriage. Preferment was in the hands of gentry fathers and guardians, so the younger or ambitious clergy stuck to the letter of the law. The outlook for the adventurer, or even the honest but poor lover, was not so good. However, the Hardwicke Act did not apply to Scotland, and some young couples ran away there to marry. At Gretna Green and other places just over the border, the system was well established, since it was not even necessary to find a priest or call banns. A declaration of intent before two witnesses was enough. Most of these runaway marriages, once the damage was done, were re-solemnised in England.

Banns and licences

Banns had to be called for three Sundays in open church, but formal records are rare before 1754. The 'Hardwicke' registers had printed spaces for banns, either at the beginning of the book, with actual marriages starting halfway through, or combined with the marriage entries themselves. The clerk tended to write down the names for which banns were to be called as requested, and some of these were not followed by a wedding in the parish, or at all. In this case, the 'marriage' space below may be filled in with a licence marriage, or the next banns marriage as it occurred. Banns may be stopped after one or two Sundays and the reason written in – usually one party was under age, but some changed their minds. Completed banns are not proof that a marriage took place, but a guide.

Some banns books, especially those used from 1823, are separate from marriage registers, but always worth studying. There is often a gap between 1813 and 1822, possibly because Rose Act books tended not to include banns pages. The 1824 Marriage Act ordered keeping of actual banns registers again, instead of 'loose papers'.

The banns may state a parish of origin which is not in the actual register, or be the only clue where to look for the actual wedding, in the bride's parish.

If people wanted to marry in a hurry, or without local publicity, or outside their own parishes, they obtained a licence. It was partly a status symbol, used at first by the gentry, and then by better-off farmers and tradesmen, to show they had arrived socially. It was also used by nonconformists, and for the marriages of parents of bastards. In this case, it was paid for by the parish overseers, while they had the man nailed down and more or less willing.

Licences could be obtained from the bishop or archdeacon, or a deputy appointed to serve a rural area (a coveted appointment of profit); clergy in 'peculiars' (parishes exempt from normal church jurisdiction); and, above these, the two archbishops, through their officials. A 'common licence' named two parishes where the marriage could take place, one of which should have been the home parish, but it could be used elsewhere in practice, often at the nearest church to hand after obtaining it, possibly the one from which the licence was issued.

An archbishop's licence allowed a wider range of parishes, again specified in the paper. A 'special licence' allowed marriage anywhere – these are rare except in wartime or among the highly mobile upper class.

Bishops' and archdeacons' licences and sometimes their official surrogates' should be filed in the diocesan registry (mostly transferred to County Record Offices now) and are sometimes indexed or listed (see the Gibson Guide to *Bishops' Transcripts and Marriage Licences*). Records of licences issued by surrogates or in peculiars often have not been preserved.

Where there is a filed record, you should find an Allegation and Bond, which ought to give the ages of the parties, the name of the father if one was a minor, and the name of the bondsmen, who may be relatives.

Ages are not totally reliable. Minors might claim they were over 21 and ages may be given as '21 and upwards', '30 and upwards', which could be a long way upwards, especially for second marriages. The bond was forfeit if the information sworn was wrong or the marriage was not performed, though I have no evidence that this happened if the parties changed their minds rapidly. The actual licence was handed by the groom to the clergyman, and only rarely survives, if it happened to be tucked into a register or the parish chest.

Many gentry holders of licences obtained them so that they could marry in London, or a town convenient for their friends to gather. Their range of 'marriage horizon' tended to be wider, so that they had to allow for relatives travelling some distance. This makes pre-1754 marriage difficult to trace and emphasises the importance of marriage indexes.

Quakers and Jews

Because of the difference in their ceremonies and the very much better record keeping, Quakers and Jews were exempt from the provisions of the Hardwicke Marriage Act. The Sephardic Jewish marriages have been published to 1837 and the Ashkenazi marriage records are held by the United Synagogue, Woburn House, Upper Woburn Place, London WC1H 0EZ for the Dukes Place Synagogue, and the Western Synagogue's at Crawford Place, London W1H 1JD. Non-London synagogues should be approached direct (see also *My Ancestor was Jewish*).

The Society of Friends (Quakers) operated a much stricter system than the Church of England, investigating at length those who applied to marry to make sure they were in good standing and not in any way involved with anyone else. The marriage took place before the whole Meeting, and the registers give the names of the parties, the occupation of the husband, their residence, the name of both parents of each, and the residence of the parents –which is better than any Anglican register, even after 1837. The couple signed, then more or less all those present, starting with relatives.

All Quaker registers had to be handed in to the Registrar General in 1837 (with other nonconformist registers) and are now at the Family Records Centre, 1 Myddleton Street, Islington, London EC1R 1UW. However, before they were deposited, a complete digest was made, with an alphabetical index for each Meeting area. This includes the parents' names of the person indexed, and it is necessary to check both parties for the complete family information. Witnesses' name can only be found in the original registers. Some County Record Offices hold film copies of their local nonconformist registers, including Quakers'. They cover the period from the mid 17th century to 1837. Digests for the whole country may be found at Friends' House, Euston Road, London NW1 2BJ, and consulted for a modest fee. There are similar digests and registers of births and deaths (see *My Ancestors were Quakers*).

Nonconformists and Catholics

There was no legal way for Protestant or Catholic dissenters to marry in their own faith after 1754. Catholics tended to wed secretly before their priest and then again in the parish church, especially where property was at stake. Methodists married in church without much problem, since they originally thought of themselves somewhat as a reforming group of the Church of England. Baptists and Independents sometimes continued to 'marry' at their meeting, but this was liable to cause problems for their children. If they went to the local parish church, where they were known, the gleeful parson often tried to force baptism on them as a condition for performing marriage. Instances are recorded of the unwilling postulant making obscene gestures or turning his back at the last minute, and having quite the wrong part of his anatomy signed with the cross.

It was possible to avoid this indignity by getting a licence and going to a distant parish. There were still some which had the right to issue their own licences. Churches in large towns were much less fussy about the religious condition of their couples, and those who could afford to get to St George's, Hanover Square or St Marylebone in London, or Plymouth, Portsmouth, Birmingham or Manchester in the provinces still found a 'two chairs, no waiting ' attitude.

The 18th century registers

Apart from marriage registers after 1754, there was no set form for keeping registers. There was a legal requirement, from 1598, that the books had to be parchment, but parchment cost money. Often you will find a statement that the Reverend Mr X, or two named churchwardens, had paid so-and-so for the purchase.

Some of the smallest parishes made do with a little book of very poor quality. Large parishes may have separate books for baptisms and burials, especially in later years. Sometimes the registers record events mixed as they happened, but more usually they divide up the baptisms, marriages and burials. Often the baptisms are at the front of the book, the burials starting at the other end, by turning the book upside down, and the marriages (to 1753) in the middle. Space may have run out for the baptisms, so they were tucked in on half pages among the marriages, or started again in the 'burial' end of the book. If you are searching one of these registers, make sure you find all the years, noting if you miss some. If the registers are in a Record Office, they should catalogue exactly what is in the register, so check if there seems to be a gap. Sometimes there really is a gap, where a page has fallen out of the register long ago, or been torn out later, or where the parson left a space to copy in some of the events when he had time, and never did. There may be a bishop's transcript to cover this gap.

It was entirely up to the clerk or clergyman what form his entry took. Usually by this stage, the full date of baptism, the name of the child and the Christian names of father and mother are given. But frequently in the north only the father's name was stated. This caused obvious problems when questions of inheritance arose, since there were endless duplications of names like 'John Thorpe' or 'Joseph Rhodes'. Perhaps to counteract this, in 1777 the Archbishop of York suggested that improvements should be made in the amount of detail in registers, and, notably in the deanery of Doncaster, this was zealously done. For a period of ten years or so, baptismal entries gave full details of the mother, her maiden name, and, for a time, included the occupation of the father, his residence, the name of his father and his wife's, and their residences, and even the child's position in the family ('fourth child and second son of'). This is a family historian's dream where it occurs.

There was a general tendency as the century wore on to add more detail to the registers, especially where a clergyman had been resident a long time and knew his parishioners well. The mother's maiden name appears in baptisms fairly often in the 1790–1812 period, not necessarily for many years at a stretch. Father's occupation may be given, particularly if there are two couples named, eg John and Mary Harris, in the same parish. If both are labourers, one may be described by his seniority, or his residence. Occasionally, dates of birth may be included for a while. It is entirely at the whim of the clergyman concerned.

There is often extra detail in burials. Here again, entirely at the whim of the clergyman, there may be occupations, ages, locations, the name of the father of a child or the husband of a woman. There are sometimes comments on the character of the late not necessarily lamented. As many people could not read nor write, the comments are uninhibited by the laws of libel or fear of retribution. For the literate part of the congregation, the comments may be in Latin, Greek, French or even personal shorthand. There may be less rude comments which are useful for family history: 'he married the daughter of Mr Jones of Newton', 'the first that ever sowed sainfoin in these parts', or 'his family came out of Scotland'.

Some of the clergy were interested in medical matters, and give causes of death – almost always if there is an epidemic of plague or fever. Although it was mainly the country clergy who had the leisure to do this, the cause of death is recorded consistently for some years in busy town parishes like St Mary Whitechapel, and Sheffield. There are sad stories of whole families dying within a month of some contagion.

Strangers dying in a parish may have their place of origin given (probably in hope of recovering the cost of burial). If any of these are spotted, it is helpful to note them and send them to the Family History Society of the home area.

The printed registers of 1813 leave little space for comments and additional remarks, so that there was a loss of detail in a number of parishes.

From 1783 to 1794 you will notice in burial registers 'pd 3d' or 'P' against entries. A tax of threepence was imposed on all entries registered, unless the person was too poor to pay. The clergy resented being used as unpaid tax collectors, so they tended to let anyone who did not appear on a tax-paying list off the payment and set them down as 'P' for pauper. The note 'pd 3d' indicates that the person was well off, or uncommonly law-abiding.

Chiddingly
Births & Baptisms
1787.

S: Names		Born	Bapt:
Guy	John, Son of Walter & Ann Guy	Dec.r 18.86	Jan.ry 8.4
Ellis	Sarah, Dau.r of Henry & Lucy Ellis	Dec.r 22.86	Jan.r 8.
Willard	Catherine, Dau.r of Jo.n & Ann Willard	Nov.r 26.86	Jan.r 29.
Thorpe	Ann, Dau.r of W.m & Ann Thorpe	Jan.ry 17.	Feb.r 2.
Oliver	Phillis, Dau.r of Tho.s & Eliz.th Oliver	Oct.r 9.86	Feb.r 11.
Willey	Keziah, Dau.r of John & Mary W.y Travellers	Feb.r 28.	March 11.

Eighteenth century registers
Above: an example of a Baptism register also giving dates of birth.
Below: the standard form of Marriage register introduced by the
Hardwicke Act from 1754. The lower example is from Gt. Marlow, Bucks.

N.o William Barnett — — — — of this Parish
Batchelor — And Ann Healey of this parish
Spinster — — — — — — — were
Married in this Church by Banns — — — —
this Eigth — Day of June in the Year One Thousand seven Hundred
and Seventy Eight By me John Lewis Curate
This Marriage was solemnized between Us { The + mark of W.m Barnett
The + mark of Ann Healey
In the Presence of { S. Percy J. Lawes
J. Mopenton

N.o Edward Compton Widower & Mary Stockbridge Spinster of this Parish
— — — — — — —
— — — — — were
Married in this Church by Licence
this 21.st Day of June in the Year One Thousand Seven — Hundred
and Seventy eight — By me J. Cleobury Cur.t
This Marriage was solemnized between Us { Ed.d Compton
Mary Stockbridge + her mark
In the Presence of { Docter Stacey
Hannah Stacey

The name of a person with property is often underlined and/or the word 'Mortuary' added. This means that the clergyman had claimed from the executors the customary fee of ten shillings for an estate worth £40 or over, which had been a legal fee in Tudor times. Anyone labelled 'Mr' is a gentleman, a rich man, or one worthy of honour in the parish. 'Mrs' is similarly used to indicate social status, not necessarily for a married lady. The infant children of the Squire are called 'Mr' and 'Mrs' from baptism.

There may also be a fee for 'breaking the ground', payable for the first of a family of incomers buried in the churchyard, after which subsequent members had the right to burial. If a couple moved away temporarily but were still legally settled in the parish, they might send their babies back to be buried at 'home'. There was an extra fee for the burial of a non-settled person, even if he wished to be buried in the parish because distant ancestors came from it. Burial in the church itself cost even more, and is a distinct status symbol.

Old Style – New Style

Before 1752, the year began on March 25 in church registers, which is why a baby can be born in December and baptised in January the same year. When you are copying entries from registers before this date, for dates between January 1 and March 24, get into the habit of writing down the 'old style' date **and** the new one. If the register says '14 January 1714' then it is 1715 in modern times. But if you correct it then and there, some time later you may wonder if the date is new-style 1715, or really 1716. So write down '14 Jan 1714/5', then you will know just what was intended.

This calendar reform was decreed by the Pope in 1582, and you will find some clergy using 'new style' then, but they were soon brought to heel and reverted, though some mutinously described it as 'after the style of the church of England'. In Scotland, 'new style' was adopted in 1600, which could be important if you are working near the border even in England.

Quakers, oddly, followed church usage in naming their months. They did not use pagan names, but began their year in March as 'first month', so that, for instance, 7th month exactly translates the Latin 'September', 10th month is December, and so on.

At the same time as this reform in 1752, the calendar was corrected by the removal of eleven days (3–14 September), for the world had 'run fast' by that amount over the centuries. People with birthdays after 2 September sometimes adjusted the date, which is why printed biographies may not tally with birth/baptism dates you find in registers.

The loss of eleven days was adjusted for in leases, and families no doubt had their own arrangements about missing birthdays, but the eleven days can make a difference to calculations of age around this period. You will occasionally find people referring to 'old Michaelmas', or 'old Christmas Day'. The most enduring reminder is the start of the modern financial year on 5 April, eleven days after the old New Year's Day of 25 March.

Baptismal customs

Parish registers do not normally include birth as well as baptismal dates, but some clergy did choose to state them, consistently or for a few years. Where they are given, it is possible to work out the local 'custom' for baptising. Country baptisms in general took place at three to four weeks, the latter being more common, though in some areas, a week or a fortnight seems to have been the rule laid down by some long forgotten cleric. Severe winter weather or distance from the church could extend this.

Town baptisms, where the infant was much more at risk from infection and poor sanitary conditions, often took place within days of birth. Too often, they are followed by a burial entry within the week. The wealthier town families would sometimes send the mother to the country home for the birth.

The first child of a couple might be born at home with Mum, or be brought back to the mother's house for baptism. Some couples who moved to town, and perhaps ceased to attend church, might have the babies baptised when they came home on a visit to the grandparents, which gives a useful link with a distant address, especially a London one.

If an infant was frail, the clergyman would be sent for to 'half-baptise' the child at home, followed by the formal Christening ceremony with godparents in the church later on. These are entered as 'private baptism', 'at home' (or 'domi' in the Latin period) and the later church ceremony as 'received into church', or 'RIC'. In dire emergency, the midwife could baptise the child – in which case, the only register entry is likely to be a burial soon after. If, against expectation, the baby survived, the register may record that the midwife gave the wrong name, even one of the wrong sex in rare cases, or, in the early days, played safe and named the child 'creature of God'. By the early 1800s, private baptism had a certain social cachet in some areas, and the gentry and rich farmers used to send for the parson as a matter of course rather than necessity.

Extra names can be added at baptism, or the original name altered. There is provision for baptismal names to be added to a birth certificate within a year of registration, though this is rarely formally done. Nowadays, we all know someone who has taken against the name they were originally given and is known for all purposes by a different one, which can cause problems of proving identity or tracing ancestry. It did happen occasionally in earlier centuries, but is difficult to prove, though well-documented cases of 'Mercy' and 'Honor' becoming Mary and Hannah, after breaking with the chapel, or baptised Edmunds becoming Edwards (and vice versa) are known. Ann and Agnes, Jane and Joan, Mary Ann and Marion, Betty and Elizabeth, are always recognised variants of the same name.

It is never safe to assume that a multiple baptism is one of twins, triplets . . . sextuplets, unless it fills a regular two-year slot in the family. More often, it will be that of a family of nonconformists who have seen the light, willingly, or because they were forced to it to claim parish relief. Sometimes the clergyman will state the age of children above infancy, or even older than the norm of weeks for the parish. Nonconformist parents might bring a sickly baby to church, with a kind of superstitious feeling that conformity might save its life. For the poor, it might be a condition of receiving treatment from the doctor paid by the parish.

A marriage followed by a (perhaps rapid) first baptism, a second in about a year, and others at two or two-and-a-half year intervals, with the last child after a longer gap, extending over a period of 20-odd years, is a 'complete' family. There are endless variations but a break in the pattern may mean a move to another nearby parish, or a period of local or personal malnutrition.

Infant mortality was very high, and it was customary to name a succession of sons with one name until one survived. Very occasionally, where a legacy hung on having a son named Thomas, and the current incumbent was sickly, a second baby might be given the name as well. In ordinary families, duplication rarely occurs at all, and then mainly in a second family, after the first family are married and away.

In the earlier registers, some babies who died were designated 'chrisomers'. In some places, this has the strict meaning of a baby baptised, and wrapped in a chrisom cloth, but dying before the mother was 'churched' at six weeks after the birth. In other places, it referred to any baby dying after birth but before baptism, still in swaddling bands and technically unnamed.

Double names are rare before 1660 and then occur at first mostly in gentry families. 'Posthumous' as a second name for a child born after the father's death is met. Courtiers added the monarch's name to their son's first name – with curious effect in the time of Queen Anne for William Anne Keppel. Double-naming slowly spread down the social scale, but at any time before 1800 in town and 1830+ in the country it may indicate social status or ambition. The upper classes retaliated by giving triple or quadruple names as the custom spread. A surname used as second forename may imply hopes of inheritance from the person whose name is used, but far more often indicates illegitimacy.

Illegitimacy

There are a number of expressions found in parish registers denoting bastardy. These are fully listed in the chapter on Illegitimacy. They are normally obvious – base, spurious, 'son of the people' are common terms. In many of the older registers the father's name is stated too. If he is called 'reputed' it means that paternity was certainly known; if 'imputed' that he has been accused but it hadn't finally been settled (on the other hand, if the parson had had any doubt, he wouldn't have used the name). As mentioned, paternity could be shown when naming the child by using the father's name as well.

Burials in woollen; 'Collectioners'

In 1666 and again in 1678, the flagging wool trade was encouraged by a law that all corpses could be buried 'in sheep's wool only', on pain of a fine payable to the poor box. The gentry still used silk or linen shrouds, and it seemed to be a point of honour for all of them, magistrates as well, to break the law in this way, rather than 'cheat the poor men's box'.

The relatives or friends of every deceased person had to swear an oath before the local JP or a clergyman of another parish that the body had been 'buried in woollen' within eight days, and this may be written in a special book, or simply recorded in the ordinary burial register as 'affidavit', or 'afadavy', or 'Aff' against the name.

The word 'Collectioner' or 'Collr' is sometimes added to names in the burials. This means that the deceased was in receipt of parish relief, collected from the better-off as poor rate.

Missing burials

Occasionally, there is no trace of the burial of an infant, though he is replaced by another of the same name. Possibly the little body was slipped in the coffin of a relative, to save a fee. Possibly the corpse was buried on land belonging to the family. Small bones were frequently discovered in fields in the Second World War, when new ground was broken for planting. A young wife dying in childbirth of her first infant is sometimes taken back home for burial with her own family. The death of paupers may be recorded in detail in the overseers' accounts. Adults may die on a journey and money may not have been available for them to be brought home. Husbands sometimes vanished from home (which may be commented on in the overseer's accounts) and it was accepted even by the clergy that a woman deserted, with no news of her husband for seven years, might marry again. Rarely, the delinquent returns in old age to reclaim his home comforts.

Nonconformists and clandestine marriages

Often, the only trace of a family is a marriage, followed by a few burials, and then a new generation of marriages 20-odd years later. If you meet this, you may have nonconformists on your hands. Sometimes the clergyman forced a baptism as a condition of marriage, in which case it will be on the same day or very near the day of marriage.

The really determined Dissenter might marry before his own folk at the meeting, making a declaration of intent first. This was more or less legal until 1753 under common law, and certainly so if the pastor involved had Anglican orders. Quakers, Jews and Catholics married in their own assemblies without a qualm. Ordinary Protestant Dissenters mixed more with the general populace and were more vulnerable to moral pressures. If they owned any property, or their families did, they would often feel it was safer to marry in a church. The local parish church was out – it left them open to teasing, forced baptism and other indignities.

Every county had churches and isolated (Anglican) chapels known as 'places of resort' where the clergyman would marry anyone to anyone if they crossed his palm with silver. Often these were tiny parishes with little income of their own. In Buckinghamshire, a parish with a total population of 20–25 had an average of 23 marriages a year, and similar examples were found all over the country. Some of these clergy seem to have laid in a job lot of licences, which they issued at cut rates to all comers. There is a testy complaint that one un-sporting groom had 'come with his own licence', thus cutting retail profits. Londoners, even, came out to country parishes, and countrymen went up to town, to places like St James', Dukes Place, where this easy-going attitude prevailed, to the extent of 30 to 40 marriages a day. Ecclesiastical sanctions were brought against some of the London clergy who had most offended, which left the way clear for the non-beneficed marriage-mongers. The parish clergy could do little against them, and even threats of imprisonment were to no avail, for most of them were already prisoners.

Younger sons of gentry often took orders while they were at university without any intent to serve a benefice, with the idea that if a fat family living became vacant when they were ready to settle down, they would be qualified. Meanwhile, they pursued the common rackety course of life of gentlemen of the time, and often ended up in debt, and in a debtors' prison, of which the most famous was the Fleet in Faringdon Street. Originally, marriage took place inside the prison, and when this was stopped, the debtor-clergy obtained permission to live just outside it, in the 'Rules or Liberties' of the Fleet. Here the parsons would marry anyone for a fee, day or night, and they did a roaring trade with sailors on shore, visitors to London, and couples whose families opposed the match. If the husband repented of the bargain, they would tear the page out of their 'registers' for a further fee. Several of the notebooks kept by these parsons have been deposited at the Public Record Office and some years ago a transcription was started, which seems to have vanished. There are transcripts of some of the minor churches which operated a marriage racket.

Some of the clergy made ample money to get them out of gaol, but preferred to stay within the 'Rules' or opened marriage shops, with facilities for the ceremony and the wedding breakfast too, on the fringes of London as it then was. So did innkeepers, spotting a profitable sideline, with ample clergy on tap. A famous one was St George's chapel, Mayfair, run by the Rev Alexander Keith, whose clientele was massive and varied. Because of later property development, a marriage at 'St George's Mayfair' sounds classy, but at the time it was a raffish area (as parts still are).

The marriages were legal (after some argument in court) but not always stable, since many couples knew little about each other. Some of the sailors came back with another bride next leave, and one lady married two men in one day. It was quick, cheerful and probably filled a need for more than those for whom it dug a pit.

While it only involved members of the lower and lower middle classes, no one much bothered, though the higher clergy denounced the practice from time to time. But the marriage shops would also cater for the runaway heiress and her lover, asking no proof of age or consent of parents. Once a girl was married to a fortune hunter, she was ruined as currency on the marriage market. The husband could claim dowries and other sums left 'at her day of marriage' and use them as he wished. Even if she repented of the bargain, the husband would still have the chance to run through her fortune, since divorce was rare and cumbersome. It was this abuse, which affected the pockets and pride of the legislating classes, which led to the passing of the Hardwicke Act 'for the better prevention of clandestine marriage' in 1753, whose effects have already been described.

How far back can I go?

Parish registers were first ordered to be kept in 1538, by Thomas Cromwell, Henry VIII's Vicar General, after the Dissolution of the Monasteries. Before that, the monks kept unsystematic notes of births, marriages and deaths of noble and wealthy families as an aid to proving age for inheritance purposes. Cromwell ordered that *all* people's events should be recorded. It is naive to assume that what he was after was just easing succession of heirs or checking cousin marriage, rather than establishing population statistics, for poll tax purposes.

The clergy were perhaps the only local persons who could write, and the Church had been established by the King, so it was the ideal organisation to collect his required information. The clergy resented this co-option into the 'civil service' unpaid, and the further away from London they were, the less enthusiasm they tended to show for beginning the task.

The law said that all baptisms, marriages and deaths were to be written down in a book after service on Sunday evenings, in the presence of the churchwardens. In the country, these men were possibly illiterate, and had their farm animals to see to, Sunday or not, so the task tended to be put off till later. The fall of Cromwell in 1540 removed pressure from the centre, and in many places it was not until reminders in 1558 that they got started at all. Some registers appear to have been kept on loose paper sheets, and this caused concern to the all-seeing eye of Elizabeth I.

In 1597, it was ordered that all existing registers were to be copied into 'fair parchment books', at least from the beginning of her own reign. In large parishes, this was a mammoth task. Wealthy clergy coped by hiring a scrivener to do the work. The less affluent might buckle to and do the job as intended, and some unwary searchers have been known to swear that the same clergyman was in a certain parish for 60 or more years, led astray by the same writing for years in this copy register. Some clergy started their task at 1558, ignoring what had gone before. Some started manfully, and then either eased their task by cutting down the wording to the bare minimum, or left out parts of years or even a stretch of ten or 20 years. If the number of events per year drops suddenly from 20 to three, or there is a gap, you can suspect the clergyman's energy, rather than that all his parishioners suddenly stopped giving birth (or even stopped dying). Rarely, the original paper register has survived and comparison can be made, showing neglect.

Christmass : 1643

[handwritten baptism register entries, 1643]

Well-maintained **seventeenth century registers** at Chiddingly, Sussex.

Above: Baptisms, with prominence from larger, lettering for those considered important, such as the parson's daughter Anne.
Below: Burials, with that of a centenarian and other supplementary information.

Anno Dñi. 1645.

Mary Burges ye daughter of Nicolas Burges was bur. Apr. 11th
James Tickhurst servant to Rich: Miller was buryed, Apr. 15th
    Here came in the Directory.
Thomas Gouldings was buryed, May. 6th
Dorothy Earle (a woman of a great age, viz: 106.) was buryed, May. 25
Thomas Harmar, a litle child was buryed, June 3.
Richard Page an Infant was buryed, June. 28.
Joane Sims ye wife of Thomas Sims was buryed, Aug. 12.
Edward Quickhampton a litle child was buryed, Sept. 10th
Catherine a base borne child of Phineas Payne was buryed, Sept. 14th

What details are given?

There was no rule about the precise form the entries should take. It was entirely up to the clergyman whether he chose to record:

Baptysed John son of John Smithe

Baptised John Smyth sunn of John Smith

Baptised John ye sonne of Joh. and Marie Smytthe

Baptised John Smith ye secant soone of John Smythe ye carpenter and of Marie his wyf

or just

Baptised Joh. Smith

The first form is by far the commonest, since mere mothers were not important.

Marriages normally record only the names of the couple:

John Smith married Mary Brown

but sometimes the event is entered merely as:

John Smith married Mary

or even

John Smith married his wyf.

Both baptismal and marriage entries tend to name mother or wife more often as time goes on.

Burial entries may give the name only, but often extra information is added. Children may be labelled with their father's name and wives with their husband's – though sometimes the entry is for:

ye wyf of John Smith

without further name stated. If other entries read this way, then probably a male name without further description is an adult. If anyone attained a great age (over 75 was antique) this may be stated:

Buried John Brown of the age of 90 yeres as he sayth.

Deaths of the gentry or the clergyman's own kin are sometimes writ large, followed by a eulogy, in English or Latin. But less exalted persons may have their own memorial:

Buryed Solomon Sotherden an honest miller: there be not many such

Rychard Snatchell, a stout young man, a curious blacksmith died of ye smallpoxe and was buried the last day of Maye [1643]

Buried Mary West strumpet to John Harris.

As mentioned above, early registers sometimes have entries mixed together, sometimes written up at the end of the year with baptisms, etc, grouped together, sometimes with baptisms, marriages and burials in separate sections of pages – always check.

Clerk's rough books

Sorting of the registers was made possible because the parish clerk kept a rough Day Book in which events were entered as they occurred. These were then copied out into the 'fair register' by the clerk himself or the parson, at intervals, and, in small parishes, sometimes only at the end of the year, as above. If the clerk wrote badly, scribbled entries on loose sheets of paper, or lost his book during the year, there were errors or omissions in the final record. Where rough books survive (as in Banbury, Oxfordshire) it is possible to spot these, but most books probably were kept in the clerk's hands and possibly destroyed when they were full. Even where they do survive and give an obviously more accurate statement of affairs, they are not legal evidence, any more than are bishop's transcripts.

In town parishes, the clerk was a full-time and important official. Originally, he would have been in minor orders and have played a great part in the service, reading lessons and singing masses, acting as choirmaster and schoolmaster too. The clerical functions were whittled down, but the clerk carried out the functions of a secretary, accounts clerk, straight man and bouncer; he kept the rough registers and usually made the fair copies; collected fees, wrote lists of banns for the parson to read out, staved off importunate parishioners and arranged 'house calls' to the sick and dying; he led the hymns and psalms and intoned responses in church, noted absentees from services, accompanied the minister on official business and so on.

The country parish did not provide enough trade for a full-time clerk, so generally the job was doubled by the schoolmaster (if there was one) or a local shoemaker or tailor who happened to be able to read and write, if he was not hurried. In this case, a good singing voice was probably the main consideration. Country clerks may have a good, round handwriting, but spelling that is gallant rather than accurate ('Meary', 'Tommus', 'Pernalerpay'); some write with hands more accustomed to the bradawl, or as with a pitchfork dipped in manure. But if the clergyman himself takes on the task of writing the 'fair copy', you may be faced with educated but crabbed orthography, and aggressive use of Latin.

Errors in the registers

Where a clergyman copies from a clerk's book, or even where the clerk himself copies from inadequate notes, mistakes can arise. If the name of a mother is not entered at the time, it may be wrongly given in a baptism – it was not regarded of primary importance. Frequently, the name of the child is repeated as that of the mother – sometimes the father's name is incorrect in this way. If you have a run of baptisms to Thomas and Kezia, interspersed with one for 'Mary daughter of Thomas and Mary', or 'John son of John and Kezia', it is probably a clerical error. 'Jno' (John) may be read as 'Tho' (Thomas) and vice versa, 'Marg' for Margaret read as 'Mary', 'Hannah' as Sarah and so on.

Mere 'spelling mistakes' should be expected. There was no standard spelling of names before 1870, when Board Schools attempted to impose it. If a name sounds right, it is right. You will soon forget that 'we always spell it with an H' (if you are wise), when you find:

May 6 baptised John Osborn sun to John Osbourne

May 8 buried the said John Usband sonne to Husband the miller. Usborne, Hosborne, Asburn are other standard variants of that name.

Uncommon names not familiar to the clergyman can be 'translated' into common ones and only a literate and determined man could get this altered later.

The Commonwealth registers

The style of entry was at the discretion of the local clergyman, and in the mid 17th century, some had grown very slack. They also included many Royalists, totally opposed to the deposition and beheading of Charles I in 1649, and most of these were ejected in favour of good Puritans, some of whom were better ideologists and preachers than penmen. To remedy the poor register keeping, Oliver Cromwell (2Xgt grand-nephew of Thomas) decreed that from 1653, all register-keeping should be taken out of the hands of the clergy and transferred to a layman called the 'Parish Register', chosen from among the locals and ratified by a magistrate. Some of the men selected were excellent record keepers, some were no doubt good Party men, but dreadful writers and spellers. In some villages, the only man who could write well enough was the old parish clerk, or even the parson.

In 1653, all birth and death dates were to be recorded in a book set aside for this. Sometimes the Register got possession of the church books, sometimes they were withheld. Some baptismal dates were given as well or the system reverted to the old form after a year or three.

Marriages were no longer to take place in church. Intention to marry was to be proclaimed three times in the Market Place or, failing this, from the church porch, and the couple were then to go before a Justice of the Peace to be legally joined. Not all JPs cooperated enthusiastically, with the result that parishes adjacent to a marrying justice may contain the proclamations of people from a distance away, and other places have almost no marriage records at all. Many of the locals felt that the new system was not a proper marriage, and slipped off to church as well, where clergy who had managed to stay in office wed them secretly.

In a properly kept Commonwealth register, the name, occupation, parish and father's name of the groom and the name, parish and father's name of the bride should be given – details only carried on in Quaker registers thereafter. Market towns often have the best collection of marriages from far and wide.

After Cromwell died and the King was restored in 1660, the Registers were dismissed (unless they were the parish clerks, who simply adapted the form of entry). Restored Royalist clergy often seized the books and destroyed them, then found that they had wiped out seven years of the history of the parish. The conscientious ones therefore went round local families, collecting entries from family Bibles, or dates of birth of children roughly remembered. This will not cover the folk who found it prudent to move house, to avoid retribution from those to whom they were known as 'Oliver's men'.

Puritanism did not die with Oliver, and in many parishes, the register entries of the 1660s by no means cover all the people living in the parish, as found in other sources.

Just after 1660, there was a great drive by the bishops to locate and punish any lurking Puritans and the results of this 'search and destroy' mission may be found among the Bishops' Registers. Each parish was to 'present' or accuse any persons living there who were not married (in church) or who failed to attend Sunday worship there. Many who had legally married before Justices had to remarry in church or have their children branded bastards by a hard-line local parson.

Although Commonwealth marriages before Justices were legalised after the Restoration, many local clergy did not accept this and labelled the offspring sneeringly as 'Smith alias Jones'. Marriages by sectarian lay preachers were never fully legalised, though good under common law, and although some couples persisted in following the same system after 1660. This didn't matter a lot unless the father had property, in which case he might marry formally to keep it in the family. The Bishop's Registers may list a couple and their teenage children as non-churchgoers, which helps to cover events otherwise now missing, in what is known as 'the Commonwealth gap'.

Punitive laws and heavy fines forced many families of Dissenters to attend church from time to time, when the heat was on, and this 'occasional conformity' and group baptisms, especially when the father of a family died, may be the only evidence that they are. There were still enough Dissenters around for the law to require the listing of their births, as well as baptisms of the conformers. Incentive was provided in form of a sixpenny fee to the parson from the parents. Often the Dissenters' births are listed at the end of a year, or separately in the register, and awkward clergy will only state 'a son of James Brown was born', not give him the name used by the family, since he had not been baptised in church.

Sometimes age and poverty forced a long-term Dissenter to get baptised. The oldest persons I have myself found were a pair of sisters, 68 and 70, both widowed and in need of parish relief, in 1742. 'Adult' baptisms (anything over about 14) do not always have the names of parents, unfortunately.

Vindictiveness may be carried to the grave. Few nonconformists had access to alternative burial grounds, so they ended in the churchyard:

Hurled into the ground at night with no service.

Even their names were challenged:

Buryed a person known by the name of Mary Fenn an Anabaptist.

She had been known by that name for upwards of 65 years and might have been allowed it in death.

Bishop's Transcripts

Mention has been made several times of bishops' transcripts (BTs). Irregularly from 1561 in some dioceses and for every year from 1598, the clergyman was ordered to send in an exact copy of registers to the bishop. In practice, the collection was deputed to his archdeacon, who was supposed to travel round each parish every Easter. This wasn't practical either, so generally the archdeacon went to one of a group of parishes and the neighbouring clergy brought in their copies. You may see a note in the register that all names to a certain date were 'handed in at ye Visitation'.

By no means all the runs of BTs are complete. Some of the clergy failed to turn up, and the archdeacon had to remember to chase them up next year, or to send his apparitor (a sort of trouble-shooter) to collect. Some of the copies were made on small scraps of paper or parchment (it cost money) cut from the spaces on other parish documents, or old records no longer current. These small scraps got lost easily or might be used for stiffening the backs of limp books.

The BT may be less full than the original parish register entry. Sometimes, illegitimate children were not included in the BT, and personal comments about parishioners are normally omitted, since they would mean nothing to the archdeacon. However, occasionally the BT was copied up directly from the clerk's rough book by a clergyman who then failed to make the same entries in the parish registers, so there is sometimes fuller information in the BT. Sometimes, where the registers are damaged or damp-stained, the BT is much more legible, and it always pays to compare the two entries where they are both available.

The making of copies for the bishop was declared illegal from 1641 and effectively ceased in 1645 (when bishops were abolished) for all good Commonwealth men. However, with the perverse quality which is typically English, some of the clergy who hadn't cared much in the past now copied out their registers diligently and used all kinds of subterfuges to get them to the bishop or archdeacon, risking punishment if they were found out. Some of the restored clerics also solemnly copied out the old registers and sent the result in in 1661, as a gesture, but it is pretty rare to find such alternative records for the whole 'Commonwealth gap' period.

The survival of BTs varies widely from diocese to diocese, though presumably they were compiled everywhere at the time. In some they may be found from the earliest years, the late 16th century and the reigns of James I and Charles I to 1642 (eg most of the Lincoln diocese); in others they may survive only from the late 17th century (Oxford, Hereford); some were burnt (Dorset before 1724), some reputed to have been evicted to make room for wine in the cellars (Wells pre-1750, Winchester pre-1780). There are hardly any for the Diocese of London before 1800 – and that includes Middlesex, Essex and part of Hertfordshire. Some have been damaged by poor storage over the centuries.

Those that survive are now mostly in the appropriate County Record Offices, though some have been committed to the charge of other institutions. They are diocesan-based, which means, for instance, that those for Derbyshire, Staffordshire, part of Shropshire and Warwickshire are at Lichfield, in which diocese they were.

Details of those that survive, with some indication of their coverage, are given in the Gibson Guide to *Bishops' Transcripts and Marriage Licences: Their location and indexes*.

Late starters and early finishers

Not all parishes existed in 1538. Many places we think of as ancient towns were once mere hamlets in another parish, and shifts of population due to industry or landscape changes were at last recognised by the building of a 'chapel of ease' (daughter church) and then the formation of a new parish. Liverpool was part of Walton on the Hill until the time of William III, and Macclesfield and Congleton were chapelries of the villages of Prestbury and Astbury until the mid 1700s.

London was forever developing. The Great Fire of 1666 burnt 84 of the 109 churches and many houses in the City, and this resulted in the combination of the existing parishes and the movement of residents out to Westminster and rural Marylebone or the fields of Stepney, with constant augmentation from outside. Many new churches were built in the 1720s, including the fashionable St George's, Hanover Square, and others were vastly expanded then and in the 1740s. A new wave of building followed the influx of people in the 1830s and 1840s, but in the 20th century, many churches have become redundant.

A similar pattern on a smaller scale can be observed in any of the great industrial cities in the north. At any time, a move to the next street may change the parish completely and even people who stayed in the same place might find themselves in a different parish.

Once you have established a county of origin, it is useful to get a map showing the parishes which gives starting dates of registers, from the Record Office, the local Genealogical Society or IHGS, Canterbury, (see end).

Reading the Registers

You may find that registers before 1733 are written in a very simple sort of Latin. Some clergy even used Latin after this date, contrary to law. I refer you to the chapter on Simple Latin for a kit of names, occupations, dates and expressions sufficient to cope with this.

Sometimes there are personal comments on the deceased in Latin, occasionally eulogies, but sometimes very rude. Ask the archivist to help and have a good laugh together.

Similarly, handwriting of the older registers is not like that of today. Read at least part of the chapter on Old Handwriting which follows before you start because even Victorian registers can cause problems. But, be comforted – remember that you do not have to read every word on every page, just the relevant ones. You will soon learn to recognise your own ancestral name.

Where are they now?

The majority of registers are now at the County, City or Area Record Office. They usually publish at least basic lists of what they hold, and some do this in detail. Always check in advance that they have the registers you want. A lot of Welsh registers and transcripts are in the National Library, Aberystwyth rather than the County Record Office, for instance. If you are working in London, a peculiarly difficult area, I recommend getting Norman Graham's guides to Inner and Outer London and Nonconformist registers (from the Society of Genealogists). This details what registers have survived the Blitz and natural decay, how they are distributed, between the Guildhall, Greater London and Borough archives, and where there are copies.

Despite the law, a few registers are still held in the parishes, and there can be fees for access.

Fees for inspection in the parish

If registers are still retained in the parishes, a scale fee can be charged based on the time taken for the search. Not all charge the full rate, being content with a 'donation', but be prepared for the full amount and reduce the time you need by searching the bishop's transcripts in the CRO first. Some few try to charge the fee per entry instead of per hour. This should be resisted with all power.

Because of a badly worded leaflet sent round, some clergy think they need not allow 'general searches' but only searches for a particular event. This is illegal, but persuading them may be tough. You are allowed access 'at any reasonable time' – but their reasonable time, not yours. An appointment should always be made. Dress warmly if you will be working in the church.

It is 'droppers in' who arrive on the vicarage doorstep demanding to see the registers there and then, when he is snatching a quick meal before the Mother's Union bazaar, who sour things for others. Some clergymen hand over registers to churchwardens, which is quite illegal, but done. Some are helpful and knowledgeable about the area, some are walking cash registers, fed up with sitting with you. Most will want to supervise you, which is reasonable if he doesn't know you, considering the spate of thefts and mutilation of registers recently. It is a powerful argument for depositing them at the County Record Office.

Some clergy insist on searching themselves. This is normally not a good idea, since for every expert palaeographer and local historian, you get 90 unskilled and preoccupied, from whom you have to prise out every entry. If you agree, or ask a clergyman to search for you, for more than a single entry, be prepared to pay professional fees for very amateur work. Sometimes they say there is 'no trace' there when they simply can't read it. If you can't go yourself, hire a record agent. If there are any access problems, consult the County Archivist, failing whom, the Rural Dean, Archdeacon and Bishop, in that order.

Transcribed and printed copies

A lot of registers have been transcribed in part or whole. Some were published when printing was cheaper, sometimes at the expense of the local squire. These were mostly published before 1914, in limited editions, and are very expensive if found, unless in a jumble sale or bric-a-brac shop far from home, where the value is not realised. Modern computer-printed copies have been produced by Family History Societies, and if 'your' parish is published, do buy it, since this encourages further transcription.

There was an intermediate stage, where five or six sets of typescripts and carbons were produced, and these were usually deposited at the CRO, the parish, the Society of Genealogists' library (SOG), the Guildhall Library and with the transcriber or Family History Society. The SOG also have a certain number of film copies of parish registers and have published a list of what they hold (though it is not up to date, since the holdings are always increasing). More marriages have been transcribed than any other type of register, and most of them are included in local Marriage Indexes.

Using a copy is obviously easier than working through the original, especially if there is an index. However, transcripts are only as good as the person who made them, which sometimes is not very good at all. The old printed ones were often done by the Squire's maiden aunt or a dotty cousin. Old colonels used to fill in retirement by transcribing, sometimes making extracts of the gentry names only – after all, who would ever want to trace an ordinary family? Sometimes local amateur historians have had a go, and stumbled over the writing, though usually they should know at least of the local names. Even the well-known Phillimore Marriage series has enough mistakes to make a genealogist weep.

Modern ones are done by volunteers, a few of whom are willing but not very skilled palaeographers. If you are pretty sure your ancestor should be there, and he isn't, check the actual year. Maybe he just isn't indexed; maybe his name has been misread. One transcriber I know read Knatchbull-Hugessen as Ruasthall-Ragurson, so use your imagination. Don't accept what you see because it is typed or even printed and bound in leather. Expert reading is the only certainty – but until then, better a dicey transcript than none at all.

It may be possible to borrow printed registers through the library interloan system in the UK. If you can locate the exact title in a book catalogue, they should be able to find out who has it and borrow it.

Scottish registers

All Scottish old parish registers (OPRs) were called in to Edinburgh in 1855, when registration began, and are now located at New Register House, off Princes St. There is a fee for access per day, less in proportion for longer periods. They are also available on-line from a commercial site, Origins, for a fee.

Such registers rarely survive for country parishes before 1700 or even later, reflecting the later arrival of strong central administration than in the south. There are good runs for Edinburgh and Glasgow parishes and some others before this.

In baptisms, almost all registers consistently show the full name of the mother with her maiden surname, which is useful in distinguishing families in a country with a number of persons of the same surname and Christian name in the same place. They are generally quite outspoken about whether the child is lawful, or begotten in fornication or adultery. The accompanying Kirk Sessions records, which should always be consulted, state also which children arrived within eight months of marriage and record penances for bastardy and fornication.

Marriages tend to be noted as 'intent to marry' (like the Commonwealth Proclamations) and the actual date of the ceremony may not be given. Frequently, there are no burials recorded at all until the mid 19th century. Deaths can be traced in the Kirk Sessions record by a fee for 'hire of the mortcloth' (a pall for the coffin).

All OPRs have been transcribed and reproduced as microfiches. They summarise information in a similar form to the IGI, but include more parishes. They are sorted by county, with births and marriages on separate microfiches. These are available through Scottish reference libraries, all LDS Family History Centres (some actually hold the OPRs in stock) and various other organisations.

Irish registers – Church of Ireland

In 1864 Irish (Protestant) parish registers were similarly ordered to be sent in to the Irish National Archives in Dublin. Those which had been deposited were mainly destroyed when the Four Courts buildings were burned in 1922. Despite this catastrophe, a surprising amount of the information they contained has survived in transcript, or in originals which for some reason were not there at the time. A complete list of what survives is printed in *Tracing your Irish Ancestors* and similar books by Donal F. Begley. Alternatively, consult the Irish or Northern Irish National Archives as appropriate.

Enquiries may also be made in the parishes, but do not expect a rapid answer or any. Northern Irish parishes are more likely to survive locally. Many Presbyterian registers are available at the Presbyterian Historical Society Library in Belfast.

Catholicism was technically illegal before 1830, but flourishing. A good many registers survive in fact from the 18th century (and as they were not called in to the Archives, escaped destruction), though they are generally of baptisms and perhaps marriages, but rarely burials. Many of these registers are still with the priest. Film copies of many have been deposited in Dublin at the Archives, but permission from the priest may be required unless the bishop has given blanket permission for personal research.

Of the relatively few records which survive, a proportion will be found in the IGI for Ireland.

The International Genealogical Index

Location of parish within a county, or even of country within the UK may be found, with luck, by searching the Mormon International Genealogical Index (the IGI). This is a compilation of baptisms, births and marriages, drawn from either microfilms of whole original registers for a certain period, or from names of their ancestors collected by individual LDS church members. Burials are not included, and although occasionally 'deaths as infant' are shown, this is not consistently done.

The entries have been fed into a computer and indexed on microfiche, by surname and county for England and Scotland. Wales has an alphabetical sequence in christian name order for each county, and Ireland has a 'miscellaneous' sequence, where the county is unknown. The IGI also covers various other countries from which Mormon membership was drawn, though sometimes there are very few fiches. Complete world copies are held by the Society of Genealogists and several Mormon Family History Centres. Many county libraries, and Family History Societies, hold sets for the UK or just for their own area.

Coverage is not complete, and varies for different counties, but many millions of entries are there already. The last microfiche edition was produced in 1992 and is readily available in many reference and genealogical society libraries or at LDS research centres. Many of the LDS centres are equipped with the CD-ROM version, which allows you to key in a name and scan the whole IGI for e.g. 'Barbara Willis' born 1790–1800. From late 1999 other locations may have this facility.

A 1998 supplement to the IGI, the British Vital Records (BVR) Listing, has also been published on CD-ROM and is available from the LDS for £3.65 inc postage or in their own centres and major libraries.

Not every entry in the IGI is accurate. The skills of the person supplying the information is the governing factor. The entries are stylised, to include names and dates, but not extraneous information, like occupations or addresses. In the end, the IGI must be checked against the original registers.

However, it is possible to search the county, or even the whole country, to locate large deposits of your wanted surname. Even obviously 'family' entries may be found and a possible skeleton pedigree roughed out, but this must be checked for accuracy.

Beware of grabbing someone of the right sort of name and age as yours because it is on the IGI. There has to be a very good reason why a man born in Yorkshire would marry in Dorset and have children in Surrey. Unless you can find that reason, don't claim him as ancestral. For detailed information about using the IGI, the McLaughlin Guide, *Making the Most of the IGI*, is recommended.

Marriage Indexes

Every county has at least one Marriage Index, operated by the local Family History Society, or an individual. The idea is that eventually, all marriages which took place in the county, from 1538 to 1837, will be included, plus, sometimes, marriages of county persons which happened outside that county. Only a few of these are complete, some covering certain parishes only, some part of the years only. One or two are males only, which is not so helpful, as more brides married in their native place than grooms.

Consultation is by post, and the standard fee is about £1 plus SAE. The practice is to send the marriage at once *if it is there*; if not, some compilers say no and wash their hands of you, in which case (unless it is a finished index) you could ask again a year later. Others hold the query till the marriage arrives. No amount of nagging will produce a marriage which isn't in the index – it may have taken place outside the county, outside the country, or not at all. Some compilers file all variant spellings together, some are strictly alphabetical. The details of addresses, general coverage, fees etc for most indexes are in *Marriage and Census Indexes* (Gibson Guide) though with some important omissions.

READING OLD HANDWRITING

How to start

Probably the first time you will come face to face with older styles of handwriting is in parish registers – in fact, they are a good way of cutting your teeth, since what the entries say is partly predictable. It is much more difficult to start cold on whole slabs of prose where you are not sure even of what kind of document it is, and certainly not what phrases to expect.

When you are given a set of registers or a microfilm, the natural reaction is to begin at the beginning. This is one of those rules which should be overturned in family history – always begin at the end. There are three good reasons for this: in the first place, what you know already is likely to involve the end of the registers, since we work back from what we know to what we don't know. In the second place, as you work back, you acquire more knowledge, in particular of which other families your ancestors married into – making them henceforth 'yours' to be collected; in the third place, the writing of those early registers is strange and unless you ease yourself into it by getting familiar with the surnames occurring in the parish, you could fail to identify the relevant names among so many new ones and have to work back over them again. A 17th century register can look totally unreadable, at first sight, but if you have trained on the later years you will find names emerging from the general scribble which are the ones you want.

Even Victorian registers can present some problems, owing mainly to bad writing or personal styles. And as you go back, the choice may be between the round hand of the parish clerk, with spellings which startle you, or the crabbed hand of the clergyman. As with modern handwriting, some people have evolved styles which are very much their own, with some letters not quite like anyone else's. However, we are able to read their communications now because the whole word can only be one thing, despite the strange squiggle in the middle. And this is an advantage we have in reading older handwritings – the single letters may look difficult, but in combination, they make sense.

I have included here a number of different forms for individual letters in handwritings common in three centuries – and you will at once see that the shapes of different letters may be very similar, but the person who writes the form of *c* which looks like an *r* has a distinct version of *r* which he uses. It is just a matter of picking out what that individual has selected as his own form of an alphabet.

Capital letters tend to give the most trouble, since there is more scope for individual choice. The trick here is to study the capitals in Christian names and then pick out the same letter in surnames. Sometimes the body of the word is quite clear, and only the peculiar bundle of strokes at the beginning throws you for the moment.

I have included alphabets for different periods, but these can only be approximately dated, since a lot depends on the age of the man writing. An elderly clergyman, educated in the 1680s, does not suddenly change his style since he happens to be recording events of the 1730s. Even young clerks tended to experiment with the writing of a former age when they were recording important events. In modern times, scrolls of honour have often been written in 'Gothic' lettering and wedding invitations printed in 'Old English' style. The recipients can generally work out the odder looking letters, because they know what it ought to be saying. The same applies to older documents – once you know the phrasing to expect, you can read the words. It is just a matter of breaking yourself in on the more readable documents and then tackling the ones that look as if they are in Greek at first sight.

'Victorian Vicars' and 'Shy Young Curates'

The bulk of 19th century registers are in familiar writing, and if the books were kept by parish clerks, you will generally have no problems. They were taught a round-hand style of penmanship, similar to modern writing, with a few odder capitals. The most obvious thing you will meet is the use, by persons educated in the first half of the century, of the 'long *s*'. This is used extensively in words with *ss*, like *Miss* and *dressmaker* and *permission*, and cheap comedians still raise a weak laugh by pronouncing it as *f*. It was an American genealogist who not only read *ss* as *p* but proceeded to inform a client that her good Yorkshire ancestor was a *drepmaker*, meaning that she made drapes, which is American for curtains.

Documents penned by more highly educated people tend to give more trouble. The more used a person was to writing, the less neat it was (think of prescriptions).

There is a skinny, pinched up style which reminds me of pale young curates, scared of expressing themselves floridly. In this style, the round letters are flattened, especially in *e*, *o*, *l*, *h*; *b*, *g* and the capital letters are similarly emaciated. It is as if they were issued with a tiny pen and a small bottle of cheap ink and ordered to make it last for a year.

Some of the cross strokes were not heavy enough to come out – and there is very little distinction between *u* and *n* when the horizontal bar is almost lost; or between *in* and *m*, or *rr* if the dot vanishes. An incomplete top curve sometimes causes trouble, resulting in an *a* which looks like *u* and a *d* which could be *cl*.

The problem capitals are *S* and *L*, which look remarkably similar, causing readers to claim a *Lawyer* as ancestor when he was a *Sawyer*, or to read *Saunders* as *Launders*:

SS LL   *Saunders* Saunders

and the curate's limp *R* with hardly any waist, which looks like an *N*:

Rogation Rogation   *Reeve* Reeve

The minimally written *H* with the central bar reduced to a feeble tick on the second upright could be *It* or *If*. Commonsense generally sorts it out, but I have seen *Hutt* misread as *Iliett*.

Hutt Hutt   *Head* Head   *Stead* Stead

St at the beginning of a word, if reduced, can look very like an *H*; and vice versa.

Stanley Stanley

There are numerous pairs of names where this causes trouble:-
Stanley and *Hanley*, *Stewart* and *Hewart*, and, with a pinched *o*, *Stocks* and *Hicks*. Commonsense will not help you sort these out, but a knowledge of the common names in the parish may.

J and *I*, *T* and *F* all look very similar, in all styles of writing, and the less curved they are the more the chance of confusion. This has resulted in a name originally written as *Instone* being copied into the GRO indexes of marriages as *Justone*.

Instone Instone

The more expansive style (the florid vicar) is always in a hurry, and runs letters together or trails ink across one letter on his way to the next, rather than take the pen off or go down to the base of the line before starting the next one. The result is confusion between *i*, *m*, *n*, *u*; between *le* and *b*, *gu* and *gri*, *K* and *R*; and the *J*, *I*, *T*, *F* group above.

The florid *H* has been read as *Th*, *St*, *If*. The florid openwork *B* looks very like an *M*.

Th St If M Barton Barton

The solution is to get familiar with the surnames in the parish, and then see what the writers make of them in their better moments, which gives a clue to the worst scrawls. If in doubt, see if the name occurs again lower down. If it doesn't, make a careful copy of it – sometimes the very act of doing this makes it all plain. Don't trace from an actual document without permission. Normally, you will be using film, so make a photocopy and study it at home or show it to an expert if necessary.

Compare the marriage registers, where a surname can occur in isolation, with the baptismal registers shortly afterwards. There you should be able to locate the name and set it against a similarly written letter where there is no doubt of the interpretation. Bless all the Victorian *Henry*s and *Harry*s for deciding what is an *H* and what is *St*; the *John Thomas*es and the many *Isaac*s and *Frederick*s who show the forms of those initials.

Numbers up

Figures which often cause problems to the GRO staff (resulting in wrongly interpreted certificates) and in reading censuses are *6* and *8*, which look very similar in the 'open' state, and *5*, which has only to lose its top knot to read as *6*. The curate's *7* can read as *1*, and so can a really mingy *3*.

When Married.	Name and Surname.	Age.	Condition.	Rank or Profession
	James Gates	21.	*Bachelor*	*Labourer*
*Steuber 24*ᵃ	*Anne Smith*	21.	*Spinster*	*Labourer*

d in the _Parish Church_ according to the Rites and Ceremonies of the _Est—_

arriage
is
ised
m us,

James Gates

Anne Smith her ✕ mark.

in the
Presence
of us,

J.

Ely

An example of nineteenth century handwriting.

The 18th Century

The second stage of the register usually searched will be the Hardwicke Act marriage registers, from 1754 to 1812, and the baptismal and burial registers from about 1700, which accompany them. Again, working backwards in sections of 50 years or so is recommended, so that you become familiar with the surnames involved. Before 1733, you may meet Latinised entries, to add to the problems of reading. Although the use of Latin in official documents was then stopped, you do occasionally meet a perverse clergyman who carried on using it.

The nearer you get to 1700, the more likely you are to find really odd writing, for clergy educated well before the end of the century did not adapt to the modern style. Neither did the teachers. This example of two receipts for payment of their salaries by a middle aged female and a young male teacher in 1717 shows how she clung to, and presumably taught, an older style of writing, with 'plum' Cs and a closed e.

You will normally meet with the long s in the middle of a word, and sometimes at the beginning – never at the end, unless as the first of a double ss.

Small e is frequently like an o with a large loop at the top. As time goes by, it breaks open into the modern type of e, but some writers opened it on the wrong side, especially at the end of words. Clergy may use the Greek e.

An o should be a simple circle, but sometimes you will find a tiny loop in the top, smaller than the e loop.

There is an awkward habit of leaving the t uncrossed, or making the join to the next letter do as a cross bar. To compensate for this, a final double ll very often is crossed. Here your experience of local names will tell you if Gravell or Gravett is intended.

The upright of small d curls back over the previous letter, sometimes into it. Small p is often split, with two uprights. Small c may lack a top bar (or have one tacked on as an afterthought) so that it looks like an r, but if so, r is either doubled, or has a definite top curl.

An alphabet of around 1800.

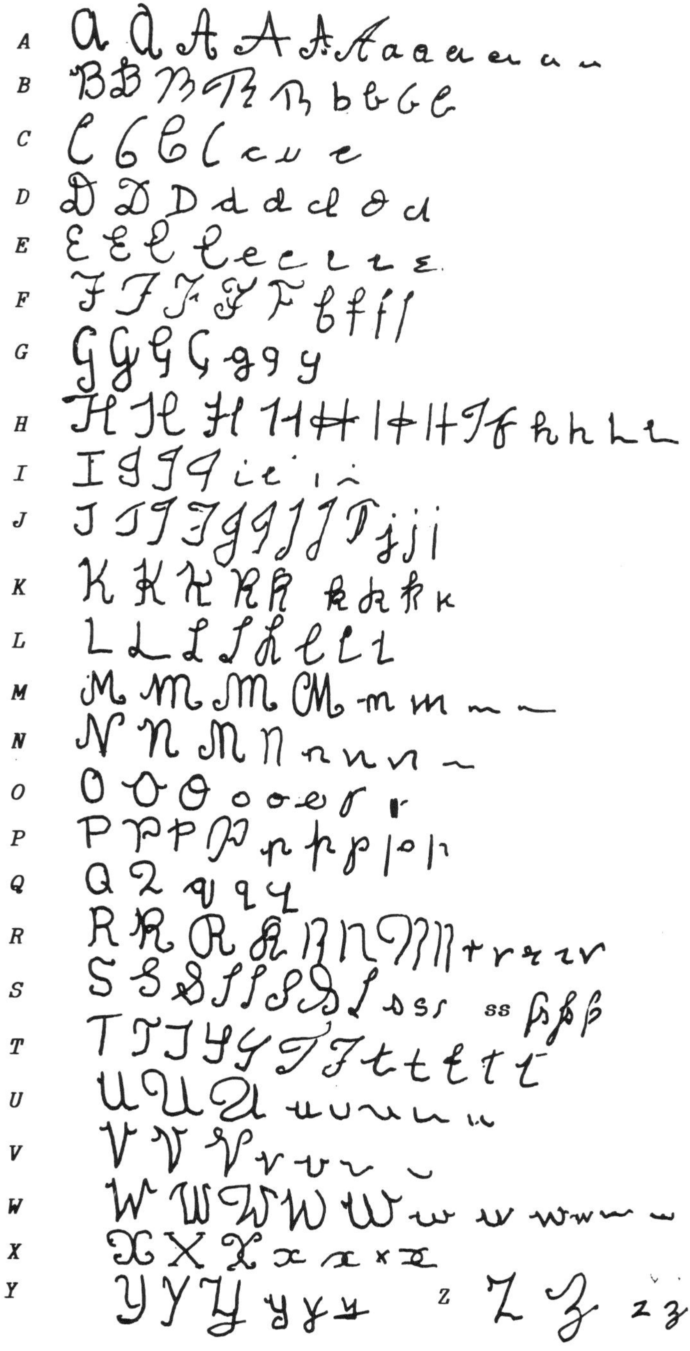

The short uprights of *n*, *u*, *m* and *i* look very much the same, and if the dot goes missing, you will have to try alternatives.

Small *u* and *v* are totally interchangeable, usually with *v* at the beginning and *u* in the middle of words.

Capital letters cause most difficulties, since they may be written in an older style than the rest of the text, for show. Refer to the next section if in doubt. Wild extra curves are added, especially on gentry names. If the letter is in a surname, check it against Christian names on the same page.

Capital *F* is frequently written as two little *ff*s joined, which causes ignorant people to adopt this as the 'correct' spelling of their name. Always transcribe as *F*. It should have a central bar and sometimes a 'top hat'.

There is usually no distinction between *J* and *I*, and very little between those and *T* and *F* in different hands. Each writer has his own way of distinguishing – if he wants to. A *J* may have a small cross bar or tick projecting left, and an *F* a definite bar jutting right, sometimes so definite it has been read as *Tr*.

Skinny *S*'s cause the same problems as in the 19th century, with confusion between *Sl* and *St* and *H*, taken in isolation. Fortunately, they usually look different in the same man's writing. Weak strokes of the pen may have allowed the ink to flake away, losing curves and crosses once there. Ultra-violet light, available at many record offices, may show up what was written there.

It is easy to see how mistakes in parish registers may have arisen. If the clerk wrote down in his 'rough book' the christening of John son of John and Margaret Smith as

bp Jno son of Jno and Marg. Smith

it was very easy for the parson to read it later as

bp Tho son of Tho and Mary Smith

and expand the name to *Thomas*.

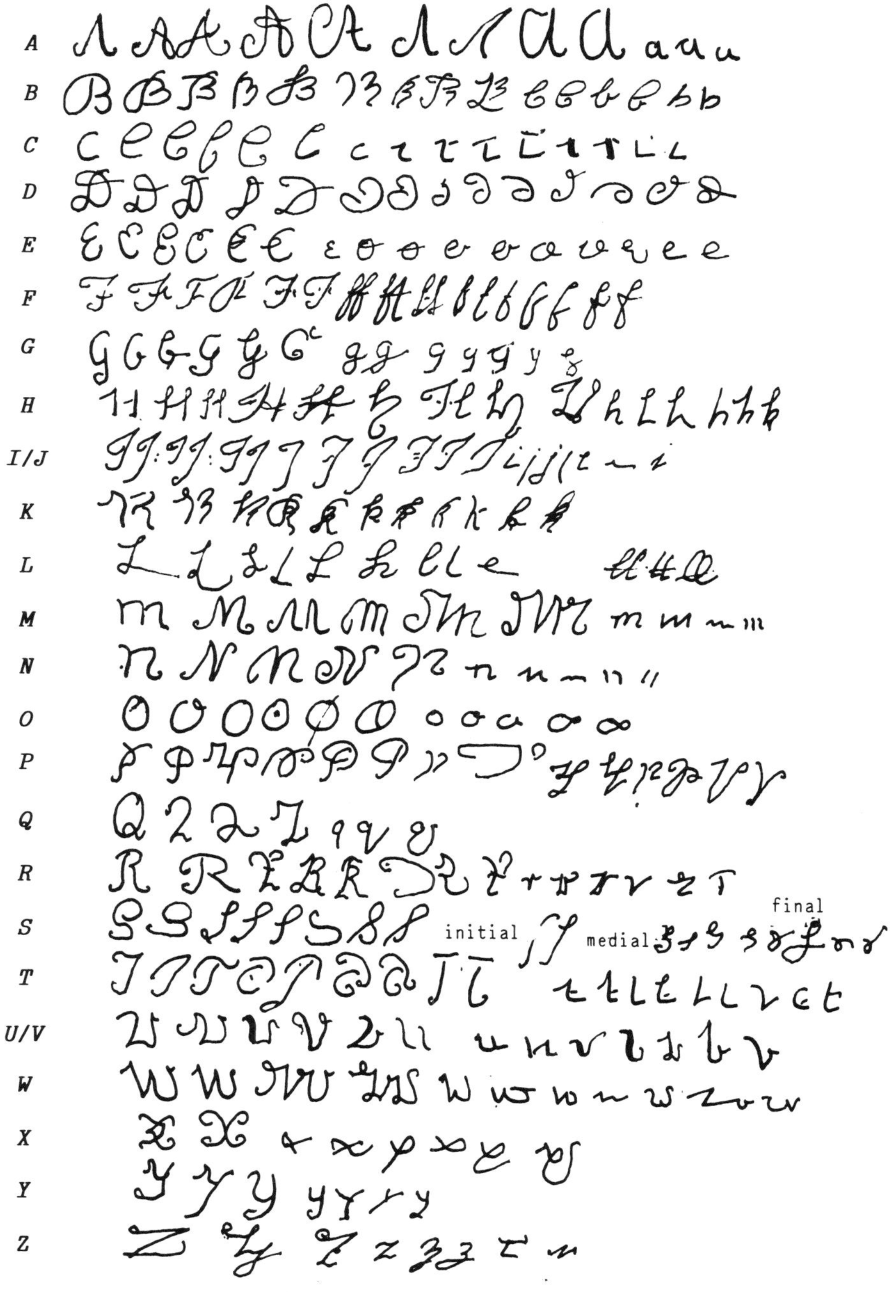

An alphabet of around 1700.

John for *Thomas*, *Mary* for *Margaret*, *Sarah* for *Hannah*, and vice versa are commonplace.

The real problem comes with the writing of those who rarely do it – perhaps just signing the marriage register. The names of groom and bride will be repeated in the handwriting of the clerk or clergyman, but deciphering the laborious scrawl of the witnesses is harder. The temptation is to ignore these, but often they are relatives, whose names may settle a question of identity. Checking with the baptismal registers to find out the clerk's version may help to discover what the scratches, apparently made by an angry cat, mean.

In some cases, when the clergyman takes over the register entries from the clerk, the standard of spelling may (or may not) improve, but the writing gets more convoluted. It may help to compare the register with the bishop's transcript, to see if one is written more legibly than the other.

The standard of writing in wills may decline in the provinces, but their value as genealogical documents is great, and it pays to get a photocopy and study it at leisure, using your knowledge of the standard phrases, with which most older wills begin, to help untangle the useful information. If there are both an original will and a register copy, comparison of the two may make things clear. However, sometimes the clerk making the copy was unfamiliar with the names of the people and places and got it wrong. Poor quality ink, which has faded, does not help, but a good photostat may improve the contrast here.

Once you know what to expect in an old will, you will realise that most of the first six or more lines can be scanned and you do not need to concentrate hard unless they seem to be significantly different from the norm. It is only when you get to *Imprimis* (at first) or *Item*, where the listing of legacies begins, that you need to read with close attention.

All swags and flounces

In reading documents created by people who learned to write from 1600 onwards, practice makes perfect. There was a very considerable variety of writing style, and it is not the age of the document so much as the personal habit of the writer which makes it hard or easy to read what he has written. There is too the condition of the document and ink to contend with. Sometimes the ink has flaked away, and it is helpful to put the page under ultraviolet light. A photostat may bring up a darker image than the original.

Although the potential writer of documents was taught a neat 'secretary hand' for that purpose and there was a modern-looking pointed 'Italian' hand in common use, the great temptation was to ornament these with unnecessary swags and flounces to make the writing look more important. It was a case of education being seen to be had. The headings and first words of paragraphs are often fancier than the rest, sometimes in an older style of writing than the body of the text. An occasional first letter is so drowned in squiggles that it can only be interpreted by reference to the rest of the word.

Capital letters are the main stumbling block, since these take many forms,

> In the Name of God Amen John Jarvis
> Buckingham Husbandman being at this time we
> feel mind and memory thanks be therefore give
> the uncertainty of this mortal Life therefore & c
> my Last will and Testament in manner and for.
> Soul into the hands of Almighty God who gave it h
> Jesus Christ my only Saviour and Redeemer to,
> from all my sins and to inherit Everlasting Life c

> his Last will and Testament are and Shall be Limited and
> Appointed and to and for none other use Intent or Purpos what
> soever

and although writers generally stick to one version per document, so that you can use the Christian name or other known word as clue to the unknown, you may get the awkward cuss who uses more than one form per page, slipping from secretary to italic at will. The real brutes are the magistrates or other gentlemen, whose writing is usually for their own eyes. When it is publicly manifest, then people can make the effort to read it or damn them.

Reasonably full alphabets are supplied here, but no one can cover all the forms dreamed up by every individual. If you know what people were taught and the way a lot of people handled this, you should be able to work out what even the crabbiest writing is trying to convey.

Capital letters (and some others)
Capital letters are looked on as a chance to splurge out, with great festoons of inky twirls and twiddles afflicting the innocent letters. The decoration is usually to the left of (or above/before) the letter, so blanking out the first section may help with the worst excesses.

A: frequently lacks a cross bar. It should be a blunted triangle with a waist, but where this has opened out, the tail of the letter may be carried across the centre to form a bar. There is an odd old-style version with an open top and closed bottom, which should have a low bar, like a printed **a**. Without it, it looks like a *U*.

B: may have a lot of superstructure or initial flourish, doubling its size, but put your finger over this, and the basic *B* emerges. However, some *B*s are incompletely closed, looking like *R*s or *M*s.

C: is one of the most troublesome, least modern-looking letters. There was a perfectly good plain *C*, sometimes with a diagonal dash, or a little curl above. This was too easy, so it was given a curved back tail, then the front was shortened, so you will often meet what looks like *cL* and a dash.

Alternatively, it was closed to make the common plum shape, with a central vertical, with or without a single diagonal. The showier writers do this without taking the pen off, by swirling the down stroke of the pen round and across the middle. The plum steadily lost its diagonal, tipped sideways, and opened up on its way to modern 'joined up' *C*.

D: is also very varied, but the less obvious forms are like an enlarged open *e* or a figure *8*. The latter is a kind of small *d* writ large.

E: is based on Greek *ε*, plus a bundle of twiddles in the middle, and maybe diagonal cut marks. There is a slight look of *C* plus spikes.

F: is commonly the double *ff* form already dealt with, though older documents use a single, forward pointed script *F* and late ones the *J* form *F*.

G: can look very much like *C*, only more so – with a double instead of single diagonal, or tilted on its side with a single stroke, but always with a definite extra stroke or curl in its lower section. One style of *G* looks like a Swiss roll in various stages of degeneration and all are more elaborate than the *C* in the same writing.

H: tends to start with a loop above the line, followed by a 'croquet hoop' and a great down curve which may foul the line of writing below. Extra swirls are often met in headings.

The small *h* can be merely the loop and hoop, which looks modern, or the loop and down curve, which looks more like half a paper clip.

J and *I* are regarded as totally interchangeable letters in most cases. If anyone wishes to show a distinction this is generally done by lengthening the down stroke or increasing the top curve of the *J*.

Script forms and looped forms are equally common. The script *J* is often dotted in the middle or crossed. Frequently found is a crossed *I* for *John his mark*.

Small *j* and *i* differ in length, but are interchangeable.

Although *T* should be quite different from *J/I*, having its toe pointing forward, in practice these letters can be very similar, in any style of writing, especially if the cross bar of *J/I* is lost, in italic, or the tail of the *T* is carried across the letter.

K and *R*: with a closed top loop, *K* may look remarkably like an *R* – in fact, more so than most *R*s – hence the mistaken reading of a girl's name as *Ratheripe* for *Katherine*. The top bar may be thinner than the rest of the loop.

There is a similar form of *R* with a more positive bar (or a smaller loop) and a longer foot curving under the next letters, usually with a stay foot to balance it. More frequently, you will meet *R* as a mean little object with a short, goose-stepping foot, jutting down or forward – the latter looks rather like another man's *p* with a dash through, meaning *Par*, though this abbreviation is generally in small letters.

At its most like modern *R*, *K* is partnered by the goose-step form of *R* – and the swooping *R* with a *K* with tangled swirls in the middle. Small *k* is a depressed looking letter, as if it has been punched amidships.

M and *W*: bring out the worst among the embellishers, partly because they often start paragraphs. The basic form of *M* is a pair of down curves or spikes, and of *W* an up-spike (*V*) plus an up-curve (*U*). The size of both can be almost doubled by initial twirls and spikes, but whatever happens, the final section of *M* opens downwards and of *W* opens upwards.

N: comes in for something of the same treatment, ending up rather like an *M*. Blank off the first section to read.

P: suffers from initial flourishes, and a prevalent dot in the middle. Sometimes the initial flourish is massive, and the loop tends to break away from the stem, leaving something like a sloppy *Y*. But *Y* always has its short leg to the left of the stem, *P* to the right.

Small *p* has a large initial flourish as normal, or a down stroke and split stem.

R: see with *K*.

S: also has similarities to some types of *c*, being made with a modern style *c* with its tail carried back across the centre. This developed to a modern *S* shape, but, unable to leave well alone, the tail was carried on again to form almost an *8*, or lengthened and twisted round and through.

T: see with *J/I*.
U, V, W: see with *M*.
Y: see with *P*.

Small letters (not already mentioned)
Small letters often surprise us by being joined to the next one at the top instead of the bottom.

One not mentioned above which gives trouble is *c*, reduced from an Elizabethan curve to an angled or vertical short upright, usually thickly written (to distinguish it from *i*). This may be given an initial flourish and joined from the top to the next letter, which makes it look like an *r*. As time goes by, it acquires a lower bar, but may lose the top one or have a flat one appliqued, again looking like an *r*.

Small *r* is generally a double form facing both ways; it degenerates into a *v*. Later it can occur also as a stick with a top curl, and this curl is used in abbreviations with *r*.

Small *t* is often much shorter than we expect, and may not be crossed, or only at the bottom. In older documents, *t* curves over like a *c*.

Long *s* is used for initial and medial letters, as mentioned, and looped *s* for the ends of words. With a projecting tail it looks like *d*, or *e*.

A small *x*, used extensively in numbers, looks a lot like a *p*, but the tail points forward fairly horizontally.

A double *xx* (= 20) above another figure expresses eg *iij score* = 60. Notice that the last one of a line of *ii*s is lengthened. The same applies to the last downstroke of *m* or *n* at the end of a word.

There is a popular 'hatted' style of writing, with round letters given a diagonal or flat tam o'shanter. This is common with *a*, *g*, *d*, and accompanied by long initial diagonal tails on *m*, *n*, *u*, *v*, *r*, and also long swooping descenders on *p*, *h*, *s*, *g*, *y* and *z*, which looks pretty as long as the lines are far enough apart for them not to foul each other.

Whereas there was in the hands of Thomas
Saunders at his entring the office of
Churchwarden for the yeare (16)72   £   s   d
delivered by the old Churchwardens   4   3   5
he hath disburst it uppon the p(ar)ish and
as follows
Imprimis to a passenger   0   2

By vertue of a warr(an)t to me directed these are in his Ma(jes)ties name
to charge and command you forthw(i)th to somon all the p(er)sons here
under named to appe(a)r at the George in Aylesbury the 17th instant
by nyne of the clocke in the forenoone each musketeere w(i)th
halfe a pound of powder halfe a pound of Bullett & seaven
daies pay for each sould(ie)r & six pense for the musterm(aste)r and
that you be then & there p(re)sent to make returne of this your
warr(an)t dated the 4th February 1663.

                Wm. Goodchilde

Examples of Secretary Hand.

Common pairs of letters bring out the worst in regular writers. They are tied together and may lose part of their normal form. You will just have to learn *sh*, *th*, *ch*, *st*, *ct*:

Elizabethan scribes and scribblers

Some of the documents written by people educated before about 1550 may be much more readable to the modern eye than those of a later date, since many official ones were written in a neat 'script' hand which has many basic letters in common with 'modern' script form. This does lead the unwary into confidently starting to search a register from the beginning, only to be utterly bemused by the convoluted writing revealed a few pages later.

Most people should be able to manage the professionally scribed registers of All Saints, Oxford, for example. Enough decoration is there to make the result attractive, but it is restrained to neat little loops, embellishing a very clear main letter, or bar strokes well out of the way. The writer in 1559 even contrives to disting-uish between *J* and *I*. If he had been sloppier, there could have been doubt if *Jacobus Ince* was *James Juce* or *Juer* or *Iver*.

The characteristic differences involve the general look of the page. There is a type of writing with a spiky look to letters like *a*, *n*, *u*, *d*, *y*, etc, which we expect to be rounded. This may be combined with the 'hat on the side of the head' look mentioned earlier. Instead of curved joining strokes, there are thin pointed lines, which sometimes fade before the rest does. The writer may add to the spiky look with narrow pointed down loops on *h*, *p*, *g*, *q*, *x*, *y*, *z* and long tails on *s*, *f* and *j*.

'New' letters to watch for are long-tailed *r*:

and *r* shaped like a *z*:

small *t* curved over like a *c*:

and *d* with an exaggerated backward loop:

Small *v* is very much like a script *b*:

while *b* is fully looped:

Some letters with loops, or pairs of letters, are perversely tilted into each other:

Double *ss* characteristically has one *s* piggybacked on another, and *ff* is similar, plus a cross bar:

w lives up to its name, sometimes having two *us* or *vs* written over each other:

A real problem may arise with clerks using the old Law Hand, which is imitation medieval. The general effect is of large letters, close together, thick uprights with few or no joining lines, and very odd Gothic capitals. This style was used deliberately for charters and deeds concerning institutions, where impressive appearance was more important than legibility, so that the relevance to the average family history search is not great. The bastard form occasionally used well after 1550 can be an absolute nightmare, if it has decorative twiddles and abbreviations plastered all over it. The 'Gothic' type still used for invitations is almost as bad, but we know what ought to be there, so can cope with it.

A   A   B   B   C   D   D   E   E   F

Abbreviations

Abbreviations are commonly used – often skied above the general line of letters, which sometimes runs them into the line above.

w^{ch} = which	w^{th} = with	af^{sd} = aforesaid
Ho^{ble} = Honourable	O^r = Orator	Matie = Majesty
als = alias	$D\overline{ns}$ = Dominus, Sir	$D\overline{na}$ = Domina, Lady
$a^o\ d\overline{ni}$ = anno domini, in the year of (our) Lord		

The *p* set, should be:

1. *par* or *per*; 2. *pro*; 3. *pre* or *prae*; 1.   2.   3.

but they are often used indiscriminately. Look out for surnames with contractions in:

Coop = Cooper   *Buckmr* = Buckmaster

Final *m*, *n* and *r* are often omitted, shown by a curved up tail. Any nasal can be omitted in a word, and should be (but isn't always) replaced by a line over the top:

shearman   *considering*

All Saints', Oxford, registers, 1567.

All Saints', Oxford, registers, 1620.

Will of Richard Webster, 1619.

Will of John Barker, 1559.

A

B

C

D

E

F

G   ch

H   sh   the

I/J   = ii

K

L   final

M

N

O

P

Q   = (Scots) *while*

R

S   final s   double ss

T

U/V   (u)   (v)

W

X

Y   z

An alphabet of around 1600.

Words regularly used in a particular context, especially a legal one, can be reduced unmercifully.

Adcon is short for *Administration* (later commonly abbreviated to *Admon*).

Words ending in *-ent* or *-ant* lose both letters:

Testam^t = *Testament;*   *Ten^t* = *tenement*   *warr^t* = *warrant.*

There is also a nasty habit of joining solitary *a* to the next word, and eliding the *e* in *thelder, thone, thother, thonlie* (*the only*).

And is variously expressed at different times by the form known as *ampersand*:

At any period, the ends of lines may be filled in with totally meaningless squiggles, to stop cunning persons from adding a word which altered the meaning of a document.

Numbers

Early versions of *1* may have a bent upright, or a lead-in stroke, and tail, which looks like a *2*, and is sometimes dotted:

The *2* is always more definite:

3 can be an emaciated figure, not much more shaped than a *1*, or dropped below the line like a long *z*:

A *5* sometimes loses its top bar, looking like *7*, or has a trailing line making it rather like *6* or *8*.

8 flops sideways, like a depressed *00*

0 may have a line through it (like a computer Ø):

Many numbers, especially for sums of money, are given in Latin:

i, ii, iii, iv or *iiii, v, vi, vii, viii, ix, x, xi, xii*, etc. *xx, xxx, xl (40), l (50), lx (60), lxx, lxxx, xc (90), c (100)*.

The final (or only) *i* was lengthened to *j*:

= *six sheep*   £2. 13s. 4d.

Signs of muddled thinking can be seen in the use of
xxj^{tie} for *21*, obviously thought of as *one and twentie*
and *2° for secundo, second*.

Practice makes perfect

The best way to learn to read any handwriting fluently is to do it. Listed in
the bibliography are various books of facsimile documents with their trans-
criptions.

Law or Court Hand, used in the seventeenth century
(with acknowledgements to the Borthwick Institute of Historical
Research – see Bibliography).

SIMPLE LATIN

Introduction

This chapter is intended for people who have never learnt any Latin, or whose memory does not retain any of the standard words which are regularly found in parish registers. You may have looked at early registers and despaired of ever finding out which strange phrase hides the identity of your eighth great grandfather, but take courage. There was the occasional clergyman who was a well-educated Classics man and spattered his registers with Latin comments on the weather and the state of his soul, but most confined their Latin to the basic names, relationships and dates. A lot of clergy and practically all of the parish clerks who used Latin before the order went out not to do so, in 1733, managed with a remarkably small vocabulary AND SO CAN YOU.

Sometimes, they used words which were not proper Latin at all, but looked and sounded impressive. I have given examples of the form in which you will come upon the words and phrases in common use, in parish registers, some of which you would never find in a normal dictionary, or even one of the various Late Latin historical word lists. I have later included a Latin will probate, with a short cut to extracting the meat from it without choking on the carbohydrate.

I have not included words from other Latin documents, for which you really need a grasp of the grammar and construction of the language, or any terms which occur in medieval source material, since I felt that by the time you are into hawking and hunting or the more obscure terms from legal disputes or manor court books, you will be far beyond the scope of this simple guide. The bibliography gives Latin word lists recommended for further reading when you have reached this stage.

Latin Christian names

Some names look familiar to everyone. As a general rule, boys names end in '-us', '-is' or '-es', girls names in '-a' or '-ia' or '-ix', and by cutting off the endings, you can guess the modern form. Some are rather more obscure than this. Welsh and Scots names have often been Latinised without reference to their real meaning, using what looks like the nearest English form as the equivalent. These are included in the list with '(W)' or '(Sc)' against them.

The use of Latin in English documents was officially ended in 1733, though some clergy perversely carried on using it after that, especially for rude marginal comments on their flock. Catholic registers were kept in Latin long after this. Irish names had already been altered from Gaelic into an 'English' spelling and the Latinisation was based on the anglicised version. I have included some of these names, after '(Ir)' to indicate that the Latin should be translated this way in Irish Catholic records only.

There are several names of which the Latin form later on became used as a name in its own right, so that the temptation is to read it as if the child was familiarly known by a name they had probably never even heard of. For instance, before 1700, all girls listed as 'Maria' were really 'Mary' to their families. Even Queen Henrietta Maria was called 'Queen Mary' in English (or 'Marie' in her native French).

However, a few upper class families adopted the Latin version of the name in the early or mid 1700s and this usage percolated downwards, without the knowledge that these names were just translations, so that after 1800, you may find sisters named Mary and Maria, or Eliza and Elizabeth. Several Latin based names became popular in the 19th century, mainly in the middle and upper classes, and I have indicated this by adding '(sep. name C19)'. The most popular names, Maria, Eliza and Anna, took root in the lower middle class late in the 18th century, as did Johanna to a lesser degree. Matilda, formerly the Latin version of the obsolete Maud, had a small vogue from the early years of the 1800s.

Before 1733 in Church of England registers, and generally in Catholic ones, all names in Latin should be translated into the current English, Irish, Scots or Welsh equivalent. Sometimes, one Latin version has to do duty for two differently derived English or Bible names – '*Anna*', for instance, can be Anne or Hannah. '*Jacobus*' is peculiarly awkward, since although it is generally used for James (hence 'Jacobites' for followers of James II's heirs) it also does duty for a genuine Jacob, which name came into limited vogue in Commonwealth times. The best rule is to think of it as James, but reserve judgement and see if the name Jacob occurs in that particular family after 1733.

Some Latin Christian names

The English versions would be what the child was actually called at home at the time. Names which died out are marked 'obs.' for obsolete.

Abbreviations

Abbrev.	= abbreviated form	C19	= 1800–1899
obs.	= obsolete name	sep.	= Latin form used as
rev.	= revived use		separate Christian
m	= male form		name from date shown
f	= female form	rare	= not often found, but
C18	= 1700–1799		awkward when it is

Adamus – Adam
Adria – Audrey or short for *Adrianus*
Adrianus – Adrian
Aegidius – Giles (*Aegidia* for girls in
  Scotland)
Aemilius – (W) Emlyn
Aeneas – (Sc) Angus
Agneta – Annis; Agnes (rare in south,
  1650–1820); Anne
Alannus – Alan (Scots and northern)
Alicia (rare *Alitia*) – Alice (sep. name
  late C19)
Aloysius – (Ir); occasionally for Lewis,
  (W) Llewelyn
Amabilla – Mabel (rare)
Ambrosius – Ambrose; (W) Emrys
Amia – Amy
Amicia, Amissa – Amice, Ames (obs.)
Andreas – Andrew, Drew
Anna – Anne; Hannah; Nancy (sep.
  name late C18)
Antonius – Ant(h)ony
Arturus – Arthur
Audiarna,-ana – Odierne (obs.), rev. in
  diminutive Odette C20
Audria – Audrey
Avicia,-tia – Avis, Avice
Barnabus,-as – Barnaby, Barnabas
Bartolomaeus – Bartholomew, Bartelmey
Beatrix – Betteris (obs.) later revised as
  Beatrice in mid-C19 and sep. name
  C20
Benedictus – Bennet; Benedict
Beniaminus – Benjamin
Brigitta – Bridget
Caecilia – Cisley, Cicely (sep. late C19)
Caelia – Celia; (Ir) Sile, Sheila
Caritas – Charity
Carolus – Charles; (Ir) Turlough
Catalina – Catharine (rare)
Catalinis – Cataline (very rare)
Catharina – Katharine, Kate, Caitlin

Cata/ivellaunus – (W) Cadwallader (v
  rare)
Cecilia – Cecily, Cisley (sep. name late
  C19)
Christi(a)na – Christian (sep. name (Sc)
  late C18; Eng. late C19)
Christopherus – Christopher
Clemens – Clement (m)
Clementia – Clemency (rare f)
Coelia – Celia, Ceely; (Ir) Sile, Sheila
Constantia – Constance (sep. name late
  C19)
Constans, Constantius – Constant (rare
  male name)
Cornelius – Cornelis, Cornelius; (Ir)
  Conn or Connor
Crispianus – Crispin (obs. 1600–1890)
Cristoverus – Christopher (bad form)
Cutbartus,-bertus, Cuthbertus, Cudbertus
  – Cuthbert
Danielis – Daniel; occas. (Sc) Donald;
  (Ir) Donough
Davidus – David
Diana – Diana, Dinah
Dionysia – Denis (f) rare after 1700
Dionysius – Denis (m) v rare except
  (Ir)
Dorothea – Dorothy (sep. name C18)
Drogo – Drew, Drury (rare)
Dulcia – Dowse (rare, obs. after 1600)
  rev. as Dulcie C19
Edmondus – Edmund, Ned
*Ed*rus – abbrev. of *Edwardus*
Edwardus, Edvardus – Edward, Ned
Egidius, Egidia – Giles (m) and (Sc) (f)
Elena – Ellen, Helen; (Ir) Eileen
Elinora, Elionora, Eleanora – Eleanor
Eliza, Elizabetha – Elizabeth, Betty
Emma – Em, Emme (sep. name from late
  C18)
Emmota – Emmot; diminutive of Em.
  (rare, SW England)

Etheldreda – Audrey (rare; sep. name from late C19)

Eugenius – Eugene (rare); (W,Ir) Owen; (Sc) Ewan

Eva – Eve (rare); (Ir) Aoife

Ezekias – Hezekiah

Ezekielis – Ezekiel

Felicia – Phillis (sep. name late C19)

Felix – Felix (m, rare)

Fenella – (Ir) Finola

Fida – Faith

Fidelia – Troth (rare C17) (sep. name late C19)

Florens – Florent, Florence (m) (Ir or very rare)

Franciscus,-a – Francis (m), Frances (f)

Fridericus, Federicus – Frederick (v rare)

Galfridus, Gaufridus – Godfrey, Geoffrey, Jeffrey

Gartruda, Gatharuda – Gertrude

Gasparus – Jasper (rare)

Georgius, Gorgius – George

Giraldus, Girardus – Gerald, Gerard

Granis – (Ir) Grainne

Gratia – Grace

Griselda – Grizzel (rare)

Gulielmus, Guglielmus – William

Gualcherus, Gualterius – Walter

Guido – Guy

Guinevra – Winifred; (W) Gwyneth; Jenifer

Hadrianus – Adrian

Hannor(i)a – (Ir) Hannah, Honor, Nora

Helena – Ellen, Helen; (Ir) Eileen

Henricus, Hericus – Harry, Henry

Hierimia/s – Jeremiah, Jeremy

Hieronimus – Jerome, Jeronimo, Jeremy

Hodierna – Odierne (rare) (see *Audiarna*)

Homfridus – Humphrey

Honor(i)a – Honor; (Ir) Nora

Hugo – Hugh; (Sc) Aodh

Humfridus – Humphrey

I = J – so see *Iana, Ierimia, Ioannes, Ioanna,* under *Jana,* etc.

Isabella – Isabel, Elizabeth

Ishachus, Isaakus – Isaac

*Ja*bus – rare abbrev. form of *Jacobus,* not *Jabez*

Jacobus – James; rarely = Jacob; (Ir) Seumas; (Sc) Hamish

Jacoba – James, f Scots name, late Jamesina

Jana – Jane; Joan; (Sc) Jean; (W) Sian; (Ir) Sine, Sheena

Janetta, Jonetta – (Sc) Janet, Jennet

Jeremia/s – Jeremy, Jeremiah

Jeronimus – Jerome

Joannes – John

*Joan*is – abbrev. for John's, not Joan's

Jocosa – Joyce

Jocosus – Jocelyn (m), Josselin (m) (rare)

*Joh*es, *Joh*is – abbrev. for John, John's

Johanna, Joanna – Joan; (W) Sian; (Ir) Sine; (sep. name mid C18)

Joannes, Ioannes, Johanis – John; (W) Ifan, Evan; (Ir) Sean

Josephus – Joseph; (rare sep. name late C18)

Josias – Josiah; (rare sep. name early C19)

Josua – Joshua

Judia – Judy, Judith

Juliana – Jill, Gillian

Julianus – Julian (m) (v rare)

Kat(h)arina, Katalina – Catharine; (Ir) Kait, Caitlin

Laura, Lavra – Lore (obs.); (sep. name C19)

Laurentius, Lavrentius – Laurence

Leon(h)ardus, Lionardus, Lennardus – Leonard

Lucas – Luke (sep. name possibly from surname C19)

Lucia – Lucy (sep. name late C18)

Lud/Lodovicus – Lewis, Louis; (W) Llewelyn; (sep. name Ludovic late C19)

Marcus – Mark; (sep. name late C19)

Maria – Mary; (sep. name late C19)

Marian(n)a – Marian, Mary Ann (sep. name late C19)

Marina – born at or by the sea

Martinus – Martin

Matilda, Matildis – Maud (obs. 1600–1850); (sep. name c1820)

Mattheus, Matthias – Matthew

Matthia, Martha – Martha

Mauritius, Mavritius – Maurice; (W) Morris
Misericordia – Mercy
Micaelis – Michael
Nicolas/-aus – Nicholas; Colin
Odiarna – Odiarne (obs.); revived diminutive Odette C20
Offylus – illiterate form of *Theophilus*
Oliverus – Oliver
Ollaferus – illiterate form of Oliver
Omfridus, Onfridus – Humphrey
Onoria – Honor; (Ir) Nora
Patientia – Patience
Patricius/-zius – Patrick
Peregrinus/a – Peregrine; lit. = a traveller, gipsy child
Petronella – Parnel (f) (obs.)
Petrus – Peter; Pierce
Philemo(n) – (Ir) Phelim
Phillida – Phillis; (sep. name from late C19)
Philippa – Philip (f) (obs.); (sep. name late C19)
Phillipus – Philip (m)
Placentia – Pleasance, Pleasant (f)
Radulphus – Ralph
Rainuldus – Reynell, Reynold

Randulphus/-olphus – Randolf, Randall (Cheshire)
Ranulphus – Reynold, Reynell, Rennell
Reginaldus – Reynell, Reynold; (sep. name late C19)
Ricardus – Richard
Robertus – Robert (also Rupert)
Spes – Hope (f) with *Caritas, Fida* for triplets
Stephanus – Stephen, Steven
Terentius – Terence
Thomas/Thoma – Thomas
Thomasina – Tomasin, Thomson (f); (sep. name late C19)
Timotheus – Timothy
Tobias – Toby; (sep. name C18)
Umfridus, Unfridus – Humphrey
Ursula – Ursley, Ursula
Wido – Guy (rare)
Willielmus – illiterate form of William
Wilmota, Guilmota – Willmott (south-west England)
Xpianus – Crispian, Crispin (obs. 1625– 1895)
Xtopherus, Xoferus, Xpoferus – Christopher
Xtianus/a – Christian (m or f)

How these names are used in the registers

In a baptism, the child's name may appear as above (in the **nominative** form), but the father's and mother's names will be in the **genitive** (possessive) form.
All names ending in '-*us*' in the nominative end in '-*i*' in the genitive:
> *Ricardus filius Ricardi Jones* = Richard son of Richard Jones.
> *Maria filia Timothei Smith* = Mary daughter of Timothy Smith.
All names ending in '*es*' or '-*is*' become '-*is*' in the genitive form, so
> *Johannes filius Johannis Brown* = John son of John Brown.
All names ending in '-*a*' become '*ae*' in the genitive, so
> *Maria filia Edwardi et Margaretae Green* = Mary daughter of Edward and Margaret Green.
All names ending in '-*o*' add '-*nis*' in the genitive, so
> *Jacobus filius Hugonis Black* = James son of Hugh Black.
All names ending in '-*ix*' become '-*icis*' in the genitive,, so
> *Fida filia Jacobi et Beatricis West* = Faith daughter of James and Betteris West.
The odd ones out are the men's names which end in '-*as*', like *Thomas*, *Tobias, Nicolas* or *Jeremias*. Sometimes they are treated as if they were female names and end in '*ae*', in the genitive:

Micaelis filius Thomae North = Michael son of Thomas North.

The commonest names occur so often that the clerks tended to abbreviate them, by writing the first syllable, then the ending, written small and higher than the name:

Joh^{es} *filius Joh*^{is} = John son of John;

Ric^{us} *filius Mic*^{is} = Richard son of Michael;

Rad^{us} *filius Gul*^{i} = Ralph son of William.

Strictly, when a person is referred to as having something happen to him or her, as when John Smith married Mary Jones, her name should appear in the **accusative** case. Names ending in '*-a*' then become '*-am*', so Mary appears as:

Joh. Smith nupsit Mariam Jones = John Smith married Mary Jones.

Names ending in '*-ix*', the other usual female ending, become '*-icem*':

Duxit in matrimonium Gulielmus Green Beatricem Brown = William Green married Betteris Brown (literally, he led her into matrimony).

The same ought to happen when someone is baptised or buried. Names ending in '*-us*' would then end in '*-um*'; names ending in '*-es*' and '*-is*' become '*-em*':

Sepultavi Johannem Smith filium Johanni = I buried John Smith son of John.

But for every clergyman who could handle such complications, there were 20 who chickened out and managed to avoid the confrontation with grammar by turning round the phrase to make it 'John Smith was buried' or by cutting off the endings. Naturally, he could claim he did this to save space. Sometimes there is such an effort at economy that all the unnecessary bits are omitted.

Rad. fil. Gul^{i} = Ralph son of William.

Tho. fil. Joh^{is} = Thomas son of John.

or even

Rad. fil. Joh.

or

Tho. fil. Joh.

You will notice that this caused the writers less problem, since they didn't have to remember how to decline the word correctly. And it is very convenient, for we don't have to either.

Once you have the names sorted out, that is half the battle. Then you will want to know what happened to them.

Baptisms

The page may be headed:

Nomina Baptizatorum = The names of the baptised persons

(which avoids any need to go into the accusative case) or the entries may be labelled individually:

baptizat, baptizatur, baptizatus, baptizata est/erat; Baptiz.

Other expressions which may be found among the baptismal entries include:

natus = born (a male)
nata – born (a female)
natus et renatus – born and reborn (ie baptised)
natus, renatus et denatus = born, baptised and 'de-born' or died
compatres = godparents

natu maior/major = the older born (of twins)
natu minor = the younger
natu maximus = the eldest born
domi = (baptised) at home
in extremis = on point of death
publice recepit = received into church

Marriages

Matrimonium solemnizat = marriage was performed
X nupsit Y; X et Y nupserunt; nupti erant = X married Y (accusative); X and Y were married
nomina copulatorum = names of those joined in matrimony

in matrimonium conjugati sunt; coniuncti erant; coniuxi; copulati sunt/erant = they were joined in matrimony
duxit in matrimonium = led into marriage
in vinculis matrimonii = in chains of marriage
per bannam/licentiam = by banns/licence

ex (archi)episcopo = from the (arch)bishop; *ex archidiacono* = from the archdeacon; *ex manibus archiepiscopi Cantuariensis/Eboraciensis* = from the hands of the (officials of the) Archbishop of Canterbury/York; *alias* = otherwise known as

Burials

Sepultat; sepultabat; sepultatus est/erat = he was buried
mortuus est/obiit = he/she died
occisit = he was killed
subito, repente inopinato = suddenly
aetatis suae (XXX) annis = in the (30th) year of his age
de mana sua (manis suis) = by his own hands
felo de se = suicide
in proelio = in battle
iuravit in forma legis/affidavit in forma legis = he/she swore in form of law/an affidavit was made in legal form
corpus = the body

inhumabat = he was placed in the ground
exhumabatur et ad Londinium portatus est = he/she/it was dug up and carried to London (for reburial)
nihil nisi lana = in wool only
in tumulo antecessorum positum est = he was placed in the tomb (vault) of his forefathers
dormit = he is sleeping
iacebat in terram = he was thrown into the ground (a Dissenter)
interrebat/interruit sine ceremonio = he was interred without a service (for a Nonconformist or an excommunicated person).

There may be extra comments about the person's origins:

Place

In hac ecclesia = in this church
in hac parochia = in this parish
in hac urbe = in this town
in hoc vico = in this village, district
in hac vicinitate = in this neighbourhood
in hoc pago = in this village

in hoc loco = in this place
in comitatu = in the county of . . .
coram publice = in public
domi = at home
hic = here
ibi = there

*Entries from the baptism and marriage registers of All Saints, Oxford.
'Annoque praedicto' means 'and in the year aforesaid'. Note the use of
the regnal year, 'ano regis Jacobi 5to', in the lower example.*

de = of
ex = from
ibid(em) = of/in the same place
praedictus = aforesaid

ambo = both
unus de . . . alter de . . . = one from . . .
  the other from . . .

Joh. Smith de Stangate in hac parochia et Maria Jones ibid. copulati sunt =
  John Smith of Stangate in this parish married Mary Jones of the same place.

After place names:

Parva = small, Little
Magna = Great, large
Superior = Upper
Inferior = Lower
orientalis = east(ern)
borealis = north(ern)
australis = south(ern)
occidentalis = west(ern)
Monachorum = (of the) Monks
Regis = King's
Abbatis = Abbot's

Episcopi = Bishop's
in partibus australis = in the southern
  part(s) (of the parish etc) **not** in
  Australian parts
Anglia = England
ex parte orientale = on/from the eastern
  side
super/juxta Mare = on/next the sea
Gwallia = Wales
Hibernia = Ireland
Scotia = Scotland

Time and number

ante = before
post = after
hora = hour
dies = day usually met with as in:
eodem die = on the same day (as the last
  event)
proximo die/mense/anno = on the next
  day/month/year
ultimo die mensis (Octobris) = on the last
  day of (October)
Anno Domini = in the year of our Lord
prima luce = at first light

ante meridiem = before noon (a.m.)
post meridiem = afternoon (p.m.)
mensis = month
annus = year
eodem mense/anno = in the same month/
  year
eadem hora = in the same hour
primo die mensis (Aprilis) = on the first
  day of the month of (April)
anno praedicto (or *predicto*) = in the
  aforesaid year
noctu, nocte = by or at night.

Dates are often expressed in Latin numbers:

NUMBER: otherwise written as:

i	*primo* (on the 1st)	*x*	*decimo* (on the 10th)
ii/ij	*secundo* (on the 2nd)	*xx*	*vicesimo* (*vigesimo*, rare) (on
iii/iij	*tertio* (on the 3rd)		the 20th)
iv/iiij	*quarto* (on the 4th)	*xxi*	*vicesimo primo* (on the 21st)
v	*quinto* (on the 5th)		and so on until
vi	*sexto* (on the 6th)	*xxix*	*vicesimo nono* or
vij	*septimo* (on the 7th)		*undetricesimo* (on the 29th)
viii	*octavo* (on the 8th)	*xi*	*undecimo* (on the 11th)
ix	*nono* (on the 9th)	*xii*	*duodecimo* (on the 12th)

xiii	*decimo tertio* (on the 13th)	*xix*	*decimo nono;* or
xiv	*decimo quarto* (on the 14th)		*undevicesimo* (on the 19th)
xv	*decimo quinto* (on the 15th)	*xxx*	*tricesimo* (*trigesimo*, rare) (on
xvi	*decimo sexto* (on the 16th)		the 30th)
xvii	*decimo septimo* (on the 17th)	*xxxi*	*tricesimo primo* (on the 31st)
xviii	*decimo octavo* (on the 18th)		

Actual numbers are:

1	*unus*	**2**	*duo*	**3**	*tres*	**4**	*quattuor*	**5**	*quinque*
6	*sex*	**7**	*septem*	**8**	*octo*	**9**	*novem*	**10**	*decem*

When the English church year began in March (until 1752), September was the seventh month, and so on to December, the tenth month. This is why you will sometimes find the months written as '7ber', '8ber' . . . '10ber', which should be read as September, October, etc, not the present 7th month, July, etc.

C = *centum*, 100	D = *dimidium*, half (of *M*), so 500
CC = 200 and so on	*l* = *libra*, a pound (weight, *lb*) or £
L = 50	(money)
XC = 10 before 100, so 90	*s* = *solidus*, a shilling
XL = 10 before 50, so 40	*d* = *denarius*, a penny
M = *mille*, 1000	*summa tota* or *in toto* = the whole sum, in total.

Saints' Days

Sometimes, mostly in the 16th century, dates are given as Saints' days. The full list can be checked in *Whitaker's Almanack*, but the commoner ones in English church usage are:

> *die natalis Domini* (or *Dni*) *Christi Redemptoris mundi* = on the birth day of our Lord Christ saviour of the world (December 25)
>
> *die feste Sanctae Virginis Mariae* = the feast day of the Blessed Virgin Mary (March 25)
>
> *die feste SS Philippi et Jacobi* = the feast day of Sts Philip & James (May 1) (the first day of the Easter Quarter Sessions)
>
> *feste Sancti Johannis* = the feast of St John (Baptist) (June 24)
>
> *feste Sancti Micaelis* = Michaelmas day (September 25)

Regnal years

In some documents, including older printed pedigrees, events may be dated according to **regnal years** of the various monarchs with their names written in abbreviated Latin, eg

> *10 Eliz;   5 Hen VIII;   10 Geo IV;   24 Vic.*

The thing to watch here is that the first day of the reign starts year one, so the '*10 Geo IV*' (1820–30) is 1820 + 9 = 1829, not 1830. The reign started from the day of the proclamation (or from the coronation, before Edward I) so if an exact day is stated, beware.

'*12 June 5 Geo II*' is 1727 + 4 = 1731;

'*10 June 5 Geo II*' is not two (or three) days earlier, but 364 days later. For a full list of regnal years, with their official commencement dates, see John Richardson's *Local Historian's Encyclopaedia*. Accession dates can be obtained from the royal genealogies in *Burke's Peerage*.

The year of his age

Where ages are given in burials, usually for the gentry, these will be expressed as:

aetatis suae xl (*annos/is*) = in the 40th year of his age

(which means he is 39 and rising 40, not aged 40).

Roman calendar

A very few really learned Classics men occasionally used the old Roman names for days. The basic days were:

Kalends: 1st day;   *Nones*: 5th;   *Ides*: 13th of the month.

'Calendar' is taken from '*Kalends*'. Other days were reckoned as:

a(nte) d(iem) iii nonas = three days before the nones =

the 3rd counting the days at either end.

In the 'long' months the dates changed. Remember it as:

'In March, July, October, May,

Nones on the 7th, *Ides* on the 15th day'.

You are very unlikely to meet this kind of dating, except in the University cities. More detailed explanations are given in *Abbott's First Latin Book*, 1880.

You may sometimes see a reference to 'the Greek *Kalends*'. A promise to pay on that day meant 'never'.

Relationships and age descriptions

amita – paternal aunt

ancilla – servant maid

anus – old woman (very rare)

antecessores – ancestors

ava – grandmother

avunculus – maternal uncle

avus – grandfather

coelebs – bachelor

cohaeres – joint heiress

coniunx – spouse (f)

consanguineus/a – m/f cousin, blood relative; any relation except parent, brother or sister, including grandchildren, niece or nephew

consobrinus – see *sobrinus*

cuiusdam – genitive of *quidam*

domesticus – inmate of the house

eius – his, that person's

familia – extended family + servants, household

famulus – servant in house

filia – daughter

filia sororis – sister's daughter, niece

filia unica – sole daughter

filiola – small daughter of

filiolus – small son of

filius – son

filius et haeres – son and heir

filius fratris – brother's son, nephew

filius naturalis – natural born son; in wills, son by blood, not stepson nor son in law.

filius nullius/populi – see next section

frater – brother

gemini, gemelli – twins (see *natu maior*)

gener – son in law

gens, gentis – (of) the race (of)

germanus/a – m/f close blood kin, own sibling

gnothus – illegitimate

haeres, heredes – heir, heiress/heirs

homo, homines – man, men in general, people (*cf. vir*)

ignotus – unknown

ille – that person

illegitimus – bastard

imputat(ur) – it is claimed

iunior, junior – younger

iuvenis – youth, about 13 to 20

liberi, liberorum – (plural) children, of the children (compare *liber, libri, librorum* – a book, books, of books)

mater – mother

mater mea – my mother

matertera – maternal aunt

maximus – the oldest of three (eg grandfather)

meus, mea – adj. my

natu maior, major – older born of twins

natu maximus, minimus – oldest, youngest born

natu minor – younger born of twins

nepos, nepotes – grandchild, grand-children (very rarely, a nephew)

neptis – (rarely) a niece

nurus – daughter in law

orbus, orba – m/f orphan

parvu(lu)s – (very) small, weak, young

pater – father

pater familias – householder

pater suus – his own father

patruelis – cousin on the father's side

patruus – paternal uncle

praedictus/a – m/f the person mentioned above

privigna – stepdaughter

privignus – stepson

proavus – great grandfather

proles – issue, descendants

puella – girl, about 5 to 12

puellula – tiny girl

puer – boy, about 5 to 12

puerulus – tiny boy

quidam – a certain; *cuiusdam* – of a certain (man, traveller, etc)

relicta – left-behind, widow

reputat(ur) – it is legally presumed

senex – an old man

senior – older

servus – male servant

sobrinus, consobrinus – cousin on the mother's side

socer – father in law

socra(us) – mother in law

solutus/a – m/f unmarried

soror – sister

spurius – bastard

suus, sua – his, her very own

unigena/itus/a – born at a birth

uxor – wife

uxor eius – wife of the man mentioned above, his wife

vidua – widow

vir – individual man, husband

virgina – maiden, about 13 to 20

virgina antiqua – elderly spinster

Illegitimacy and Strangers

Johannes filius Mariae Jones et reputat(ur) de Johanni Smith = John son of Mary Jones and by repute of John Smith (ie it is certain).

Johannes fil. Mariae Green et imputat de Ricardo Brown = John son of Mary Green and, she claims, of Richard Brown (ie probably).

filius nullius = son of none, the girl didn't say whose.

filius populi = son of the people, anybody's guess of six.
filius cuiusdam peregrini = son of a certain travelling man.
nomine ignoto = (with) his name unknown.
(*nomine*) *Richardus vel Diccon* = (named) Richard or Dicky.
ut fertur = as it is said (ie believe it if you like).
vocatus = called, known as.

Status and Occupations
(the nobility, the gentry and the wealthy)

Rex, Regina – King, Queen
Dux, ducis – Duke, of the Duke (= lit. leader)
Comes, comitis – Earl, of the Earl
Vi(ce)comes – Viscount
Baronettus – Baronet
Dominus (*Dns*) – Lord, Sir; clergyman before 1600
Domina (*Dna*) – Lady (wife of lord); Dame (wife of knight)
Dominus huius locus – lord of the manor, of this place
eques – knight; cavalry officer (lit horseman)
miles, militis – soldier (of a soldier); knight, Sir
armiger – person entitled to bear a coat of arms

generosus/a – gentleman, lady (by birth, later by wealth)
clericus (abbrev. *clicus*) – cleric, clergyman, not parish clerk
doctor – of divinity or laws, not normally of medicine
Magister Artium – Master of Arts, with university degree
Magister, M^r – master, extended as mere title of respect to gentry or the local rich man
Cives et (trade) – Citizen and (. . .) of London, Freeman of the livery company indicated
patronus huius ecclesiae – patron (appointer of parson) of church.

Trades and Occupations

In most parishes, only a handful of these names will be used – but it will not necessarily be the same handful, so I have selected the ones most commonly used in different areas.

aedificator – builder, architect
aegyptianus – egyptian, gypsy
agricola – farmer, husbandman
architectus – mason, builder, bricklayer, and (rarely) architect
artifex – artisan
aurifex – goldsmith
bibliopola – bookseller
bladarius – corn chandler
brasiarius – maltster
burriarius – dairyman
calciarius – shoemaker
carbonarius – charcoal burner/seller, collier
clavifaber – nailmaker

clericus – clerk, normally clergyman, clerk in holy orders
clericus huius parochiae – clerk of (this) parish
cocus, coquus – cook
comedianus – actor
constabularius – constable
doctor – of divinity or laws, not medicine
emptor – buyer (with specified commodity)
faber – smith, used in combination for various artisans
faber aerarius – coppersmith, brazier
faber argentarius//*aurantarius* – goldsmith, silversmith

faber clavi, clavorum – nailmaker
faber clavarum – key-, locksmith
faber ferrarius – iron smith, blacksmith
faber lignarius – wood smith, carpenter
faber rotarius – wheelwright
fabrifer/ferrifaber – blacksmith, iron-worker
figulus – potter
funerius – rope maker
fur – a thief
furnarius – baker, furnace owner
g(u)ardianus – churchwarden, guardian
gregarius – drover, cattleman
horologiarius – clockmaker
hortulanius, hortarius – gardener
hostellarius – innkeeper
husbandus – husbandman, small farmer
itinerans/erarius – a traveller
laborarius – labourer
lanarius – weaver, strictly of wool; wool merchant
lanius, laniator – butcher
lapidarius – stonemason
ludimagister – (lit. master of games) – schoolmaster
medicus/inus – physician
mercator – merchant
mercator pecoris – cattle jobber
meretrix – prostitute
miles/milites – soldier/s (knight)
molendarius, molinarius – miller
molitor, molarius – millwright
nauta – sailor (m)
navigator – boatman, lighterman
notarius – lawyer, notary
nutrix – nurse, wetnurse
obstetrix – midwife
operarius, opifex – skilled workman, craftsman
ovium pastor – shepherd of sheep

paedogogus – schoolmaster
pannarius – cloth seller
pastor – shepherd
pauper – poor person
pecuarius – grazier
pellicarius – skinner
peregrinus/a – traveller (m/f)
pictor – painter
piscator – fisherman
pistor – baker
plebianus – common man; anyone with no coat of arms, even if rich
pomarius – fruit seller
porcorum emptor – pig buyer
restio – rope maker
rotarius – wheelwright
rusticus – countryman, rustic
saponarius – soap boiler
sartor – tailor
scissor – barber
scribus – scribe, scrivener
scriptor – the writer
stabularius – stable keeper, ostler
structor – builder, mason, bricklayer
sutor – shoemaker
tabernarius – taverner, innkeeper
tannarius – tanner
tector – plasterer
textor – weaver
tibialis factor – framework knitter, stockinger
tinctor – dyer
tonellarius – cooper, barrelmaker
tonsor – barber
vaccarius – cowman
vendor – seller (+ commodity)
vestiarius – clothier
vitellarius – victualler
vitrarius – glazier, glass seller

NONCONFORMISM

Back to the Bloggs family

Searches in parish registers, you will recall, were to be divided between Loamshire and Clayshire Record Offices.

In Loamshire, Sprotley registers showed the baptisms of Mary and George, the youngest two children of William Bloggs, shepherd, and Mary, and also another two children, Joseph and Betty, who died within a month or so of birth in each case. The children of John Bloggs and Sarah carried on inexorably until 1862, by which time their eldest son, William, was already married and the father of two children. His James was baptised with his infant aunt Matilda, three days younger. John's occupation changes during the course of the births from shepherd to grazier.

William junior's family suddenly stops – the burial register shows his death at the age of 30, in February 1869 and notes that he was 'buried by coroner's warrant'. His eldest son, John, was buried on the same day with the same note.

Then comes a surprise. The marriage of James Allan Bloggs, grazier, 24, is recorded in August 1865, and the bride is Mary Elizabeth Maynard, aged 28, daughter of William Devereux Maynard, auctioneer, and the ceremony is performed by George Augustus Maynard, curate of Sprotley. There are seven witnesses, instead of the usual two. This looks like a touch of class, worth investigating.

Their children were all baptised in church – starting with William Maynard Bloggs in July 1866, George Augustus Devereux Maynard in September 1867 (who died a week later, overburdened by his names), Sophia Mary in December 1869, Harry Devereux in January 1871, Arthur Maynard in 1873, Andrew Allan 1875. Father was described as a farmer, or farmer and grazier in these entries. Then at two year intervals, came Margaret Drummond, Maud Sarah, and Fanny Matilda, and finally, Sydney Martin in 1884. After this last child, Mary Elizabeth was never the same again, and died in December 1888 of debility, five years duration, cancer of the bowel, six months.

There are the remains of a large tombstone in Sprotley churchyard, from which you at first noted '. . . James Allan Bloggs . . . died . . . June 1931 aged 81.' However, this didn't agree with his age recorded in the indexes at St Catherine's House, and closer inspection showed that the first figure was actually a 9, the bottom badly broken. This matches what the burial registers say, though he was really only 90. Mary's name was probably at the top of the same stone, but only a fragmentary '. . . ved wife of' remains.

Four years later, James Allan Bloggs married again, to Jane Gates, then 32, the daughter of a labourer. There were three more children, Jane, Ada and James. Their father is by now described as a dairyman or milkman. Jane died in the flu epidemic of 1919 and her grave is marked by a small stone, labelled J.B. 1919.

Flushed with success, you decide to search the Peasley registers for the baptisms of the previous generation of the Bloggs family, but there isn't a Bloggs christening to be found from 1785 to 1820, when a Josiah starts baptising. There is a marriage of a John Bloggs to Jane Tibbets in 1786, and the burial of an infant Jane four months later, but nothing else. This is very puzzling, but while you are about it, you search backwards in the registers and are rewarded by more Bloggs entries in the 1760s. There are several children of a John and Sarah Bloggs, including a John in 1761. Working over the marriage registers again, you find no trace of a marriage of John Bloggs to Sarah in about 1759/60, but you do spot another marriage of a Dorcas Bloggs in 1778, witnessed by a John Bloggs, which looks like the same signature your John made in 1786. An uncommon Christian name – could be helpful. There don't seem to be any Bloggs entries further back in Peasley registers.

Stuck there for the moment, you turn to the Newchurch registers in Clayshire. John son of William and Mary Bloggs was born there in about 1815/16, so was his wife, Sarah Allan, in c1818. The Allans are there all right, with Andrew, Robert Drummond, James, Sarah and three other children of James and Margaret Allan, gentleman's gardener, born while he was living at Park Cottage in Newchurch, on the further side of Mr Dennison's estate. Sarah Allan married her John in 1837 and her mother died in 1839.

But where is John Bloggs? Again, not a trace. Searching further back, there is the marriage of his parents, in 1815, witnessed by Josiah Bloggs and George Porter (their marks); the baptism of his mother, Mary Porter, is there in 1796, with that of her brothers, George and William, and a sister Hannah, the children of William and Ann Porter. There is a marriage of William Porter to Ann Gates, witnessed by Hezekiah Gates. The burial is there of *William Porter, gamekeeper to Lord Clissold, murdered by poachers in 1801.*

So where are the Bloggs? The obvious thing to check is whether they were nonconformists.

Nonconformist records

For about 200 years, it was an offence not to attend services of the Church of England, at the parish church. People who didn't go, or who left early, could be reprimanded and fined small sums. Those who went to any other form of worship could be fined very heavily and imprisoned or even transported for persistent offences. This didn't stop them meeting, in secluded places, only made them more cautious about revealing their actions or committing their names to paper.

Very many of us have ancestors who at some period were Quakers, Baptists, Independents, Presbyterians, Methodists or some other of the myriad varieties of people who wished to worship other than in the established church. These persons are known as Non-conformists, or Dissenters, terms which are normally applied to Protestants who do not attend the Church of England. Catholics are known as recusants (formerly any refuser) or specified as 'Romish', 'papists' etc.

Very few, at least in rural areas, had actual chapel buildings, but met in houses or barns, which could be registered, if the owner was so brave, as 'conventicles' or out in the open air. Lists of owners of licensed conventicles can be found in Quarter Sessions records. It laid the person open to economic discrimination and the building to damage by vandalism, so some chapel groups could not find a home, and met in different places, one step ahead of the informers who persecuted them.

If you find marriages without baptisms, followed by a new set of marriages a generation later, you probably have nonconformists on your hands. In many cases, at least before 1800, you will also find burials of dissenters' children and even adults in the churchyard, since few chapels had graveyards then. Some clergymen were so bitter against chapel worshippers that they refused to perform a service and 'hurled them into the ground'. Alternatively, their colleagues sneaked them into the graveyard at night and buried them secretly.

Strictly, the clergy were supposed to record names of dissenters' children, and quite a lot are found in the 1680–1710 period, listed after the usual baptisms. Often the entry will only state 'John Smith had a son born 24 June 1698', since Church baptism alone conveyed the right to a name. In some parishes, there are fairly good records of persons baptised or even 'buried at the Meeting', where there was a graveyard ground.

If the family got into financial difficulties, especially if the bread-winner died, then they might be forced into a mass baptism, as a condition of receiving help from parish funds. Sometimes the exact ages or even the date of birth will be stated, which is an advantage. Therefore, do not stop at the point when your ancestor must have been born, but continue forward, to make sure there are no late baptisms. These will generally occur within 20 years of birth, but I have known Dissenting sisters of 68 and 70 to be baptised as poor widows.

If a known Dissenter married in his own parish, some clergy would force him to be baptised first. The result is that many Dissenters went elsewhere to marry. Before 1754, any ordained clergyman could perform a reasonably legal marriage, in church, house or prison, but afterwards rules tightened, and the parish church had to be used, until 1837. However, some clergy still offered a 'no questions asked' service, for marriage by licence, and Dissenters came from miles around to use their church. St George's Hanover Square, St Pancras, St Luke Old Street, Manchester Cathedral, and the main churches of Sheffield, Birmingham, Portsmouth and other towns were renowned for it. This may make a particular marriage hard to find. However, if there was any question of property to inherit, the marriage had to be legal, though a few hardy spirits merely stood up in their own congregation and announced their intent to live as man and wife.

By the late 18th century, it was realised that far more people existed than were ever recorded in parish registers. Very few chapels kept records other than carefully concealed lists of subscribers to funds. From 1780, it was enacted that all chapels should keep registers of births or baptisms and burials among their members. This was treated with some suspicion, but eventually, almost all chapels started to keep these records.

Often, where printed books were used, the form of record is more detailed than that of the Church, giving the maiden name and often the parentage of the mother. For example

> *Sarah the daughter of Thomas Walker and Elizabeth his wife that was the daughter of John Wheeler was born on 7 September 1822 at Monks Risborough*
> *(Princes Risborough Baptist Chapel)*

Occasionally, witnesses to the birth are included, and may be grandmothers or aunts.

Chapels might have congregations drawn from a number of villages around (as in this case). To find a type of worship they liked, people would walk a long way to an actual chapel, or invite a favoured preacher to come to a small house meeting locally. You will need to shop around to locate the records.

Methodists are a slightly special case. Originally, they hoped to reform the established church itself to their own methods, so that members were allowed or even encouraged to take church baptism. Later, despairing of this, they separated and a comprehensive system of records was established, whereby baptisms would take place at local meetings and also be recorded centrally at the Circuit headquarters. The circuits covered quite large areas, and sometimes the records of Methodists of one county are found in another.

In 1837, it was ordered that all nonconformist registers should be handed in to the new Registrar General. Where this law was obeyed, all the records are housed at the Public Record Office, where they may be seen (at the Family Records Centre, London). Most of these have been filmed and included in the IGI. This is the simplest way to check whether your ancestors are to be found, and has the advantage of including all the deposited registers for a county in one alphabetical sequence. This is useful, since a number of ancestors chapel-hopped, attending first one denomination, then another, baptising or registering a child or two in each. The IGI entry is in index form, and there is always more in the original book.

There are considerable gaps in the coverage however. Some chapels lasted for very short periods, while one preacher ran them. When he left, they collapsed or split into three or four groups. Sometimes the pastor carried off the register to his new chapel, and used it there; sometimes an elder took charge and if there was no obvious successor, the book was dumped in the attic or re-used for farm accounts. Every now and then, these missing books turn up and are handed over to the local County Record Office.

Some chapels suspected a plot and hid their registers. Haddenham, where I live, had a large and flourishing Baptist chapel. The only book handed in was an old burial register disfigured by a bad blot after two pages. The pastor claimed he had no other registers in his hand, which was literally true, since he had confided them to his Elder for a few days. Because this chapel continues to flourish to the present, the registers were recovered and have since been deposited in the CRO. A similarly withheld register of a chapel a few miles away disappeared when the chapel collapsed early this century, and although it may exist in the attic of an Elder's descendants, it is lost to the descendants of the many worshippers. Princes Risborough itself, another important chapel, dating from 1700, almost collapsed after 1790 and was refounded in 1813. The old records had been lost, and new registers were started in 1817, though births of children back to 1800 (and two earlier) were included.

On the whole, only in towns are you likely to find early chapel buildings and written records before 1780, since there were enough tradesmen to form a wealthy anti-church lobby. Occasionally, a family moving into town will record earlier events which took place in the country. This applies particularly to preachers. Burial records, where these exist, may include extra detail about a prominent member.

Be wary of dates of baptism as Independent or Methodist. These may be the family conversion date, some time after infancy. Baptists record birth dates, so locating them in the original registers is a matter of searching through several pages for a later date of registration.

If you suspect non-conformity, and have searched the IGI to no effect, ask the CRO if other pre- 1837 registers have been handed in recently. Don't ask just for those of one village, since yours may have attended a chapel two villages away. If they lived near a border, try the next county too. The CRO should know where local chapels were located.

Another source for nonconformist births is the registers kept at Dr Williams's Library in London. This was, from 1742 to 1837, open to any Dissenter who wished (for a fee of two shillings) to record accurately the birth of his children, free from worries about whether the local chapel would fail. These registers are held by the FRC and are not on the IGI but do appear on the supplementary BVR.

It was important for men of property to ensure their children's inheritance, so that most users were well-to-do, and mainly came from the Home Counties or south. However, there are entries from Leicester, Yorkshire and other areas remote from London. Group registrations were made, some time after the birth of some children, and very little indexing has yet been done (apart from Cambridge and some Bucks entries), so that you have to start in the likely year and work forward. The originals are at the PRO, not Dr Williams's Library, and are presented on microfilm.

Other, earlier, references to nonconformists will be found in Quarter Sessions records – when they were fined for non-attendance or registered houses as conventicles. There are similar records among diocesan papers held by the bishops, to whom local churchwardens 'presented' (reported) sinners like these. A few Bishops' Registers have been published, and those of the 1660–70 period are especially full of dissenters, listed by name and including references to families.

William Monke and Thomas Monke that do usually absent themselves from divine service are now in gaol for this county by order of the justices, whether for that reason or for being taken at conventicles.

Thomas Lane and Margaret his wife for not causing their sonne called Thomas to be baptised.

Mannases Haynes and Alice Sumner his wife that they were married clandestinely by Mr Francis Treble.

If you are fortunate enough to have Quaker ancestors, then you will find superb records. Births (exact date) usually record the residence and occupation of the father and names of both parents, including the maiden name and parentage of the mother. Marriages state the name of the groom, his occupation and residence, the name of the bride, and her marital status, the names, occupations and residences of both sets of parents, and whether they are then alive or dead. A marriage is witnessed by all present, starting with the nearest relatives of the couple. Burials have the date of death, name and residence, place of burial and the name of the person ordering the grave.

All Quaker records before 1837 were deposited according to law, and are at the PRO, but are not included in the IGI. Complete, indexed, copies were made and are held at Friends House, Euston Rd., where there is a wealth of other material, including minute books and details of 'sufferings', when Quakers were imprisoned and persecuted.

A number of books have been written about the tribulations of the early nonconformists, often with a great deal of information on persons. Old chapels mostly have had histories written, which will be found in the local library. Fuller details of these and other sources for dissenting ancestors can be found in the McLaughlin Guide, *Nonconformists and their records*.

Putting this into practice

Not finding the Bloggs in parish registers, you should enquire which chapels operated in the neighbourhood, remembering they lived on a county boundary. Acquire an old map of the area, study where the roads and footpaths went and work out the possibilities. The motorway feeder road has changed the landscape drastically, so a modern map doesn't give the same idea. People thought nothing of a walk of four or five miles to find the sort of worship they liked, and any cart-owners in the congregation would offer lifts.

Via a search of the IGI, this should lead to the registers of Newchurch Baptist chapel, where five of William and Mary's children were registered.

Hezekiah Gates (the witness to the marriage of Ann, his sister, to William Porter in 1791), was a deacon of this chapel. Presumably when Ann was widowed, Uncle Hezekiah looked after them, and they therefore became Baptists. When William Bloggs married Mary Porter, he joined the ranks.

You can check when he did join in the Minute Book of the chapel, which lists applications for admission and sometimes the background story to the conversion – not 'I want to be a Baptist so I can marry this pretty girl' but 'I saw the light because I was reflooring the barn loft for Farmer Jones, next door to her uncle and heard him praise the Lord while he tended his sheep etc'. So William changed jobs as well as religion. There was a Baptist chapel in Peasley from before 1790, but the only entry there is in 1825–7, when Josiah Bloggs had a brief flirtation with the sect.

The family of John and Jane Bloggs is finally traced in Weston Independent chapel, three miles from Peasley but in Clayshire. William is their third son, fifth child, and Josiah the youngest. You find that Henry Bloggs, the labourer of 1841 in Sprotley, is also there, son of another Henry, whom you can identify with the younger brother of John b 1761. Therefore he is William's first cousin rather than his brother.

John Bloggs was evidently an important man in the chapel. They acquired a burial ground in 1810, and he appears almost last in the deposited registers.

John Bloggs, aged 76, deacon of this chapel, who walked in the ways of God these 51 years. He builded the new seats to this chapel and with William and James Bloggs his brothers made the house for the minister in 1804.

So John and his family were in the building trade and he was a carpenter like his descendants, Harry and George. You can visit the chapel at Weston, now a United Reformed church, and see the 'old chapel' (now the choir's robing room) with some of those very pews still round its walls. There is a tombstone there for John Bloggs and Jane, who died in 1845, and also for their eldest, John, (*deacon of this chapel*) and four of his family. Enquiring at the church, you are told there was a Miss Bloggs who died only recently, who attended regularly till she was 89. She shared a house till she was 80 with her niece, Mrs Um – they will let you know her name as soon as they remember. They've got a lovely place, well, so they should, since he's a builder.

William and Mary Bloggs lived for at least a few years at Weston, where their children Ann, Dorcas, William junior and Jane were born, but continued to worship at Newchurch Baptist chapel till they moved to Sprotley and 'went church'. They, walking to Newchurch, may have passed Father and the rest of the family, walking from Peasley to Weston Independents, on Sundays, and unchristian thoughts may have been thought by all. That uncommon name Dorcas has come up again, so it must have been important in the family.

Having sorted out quite a lot of the family, what is the next step back? The Bloggs family were tradesmen, apparently in business for themselves. There should be wills to help out. After 1857, all English and Welsh wills are in London, at Somerset House, but before that is another matter.

WILLS BEFORE 1858

Probate jurisdiction

Before 1858, the proving of wills was a matter for the ecclesiastical courts. This probably arose because the lawyer-clerics of the old church were quasi-independent of King and barons, so their dealings were more likely to be unbiased, or at least held upright by equal pressure from all directions. Even after the Establishment of the Church, the system continued, because it worked tolerably well and there was no simple alternative ready.

There were different grades of probate court:
1. *The Archbishop's Court.* The Prerogative Court of Canterbury (PCC) dealt with the south, the Prerogative Court of York (PCY) with the north (Cheshire, Nottinghamshire and northwards). The PCC (actually in London, not Canterbury) was superior to PCY.
2. *The Bishop's Court.* The Consistory Court covered a whole diocese, the Commissary Court a designated part of it, possibly a whole county.
3. *The Archdeacon's Court.* Covered one archdeaconry only.
4. *The Peculiar or local courts.* These covered a particular parish, group of parishes or special area.

Disregarding the last category, for the moment, the normal rules for probate jurisdiction said that if a man had '*bona notabilia*' – goods worth mentioning, meaning valued at £5 or more – in one archdeaconry only, the will was proved in the Archdeacon's Court; if in two archdeaconries, then in the Commissary or Consistory Court. If he had goods in two dioceses, then in PCC or PCY. If in both provinces, then in PCC. Rules are made to be broken, and in practice executors would use the court which was convenient to them, often going to the PCC for status reasons, or for the fun of a trip to London rather than a dull provincial town. Nonconformists were particularly apt to do this, since the higher the court, the less overt connection with the church was discernible. (Sometimes clergy were appointed to act for the court before whom documents *could* be sworn locally.)

Peculiars were parishes exempt from the jurisdiction of the local archdeacon, or even the bishop. They might 'report direct' to the archbishop, to some other local ecclesiastic like a dean or prebend of a cathedral, or even be under the control of the civil authority, in the form of a manorial court. Wills records for peculiar courts may have fetched up miles from those of adjacent parishes.

There was a fifth place where some wills might be dealt with. Local clergy without law training but with practical experience were sometimes deputed to prove wills for the archdeacon. They were the obvious persons to deal with the estates also of those without '*bona notabilia*' in their parish, to see that the right heir got the few effects. In practice, it seems that estates which should have gone to probate officially, since they were over the limit, were also dealt with locally, by the clergyman, or by neighbours, if there was no possible dispute. There are numerous references to legacies under wills not proved in any known court.

Real and personal estate

Even allowing for the vast difference in the value of money nowadays, £5 may seem a very small sum. It must be understood that the value of a will as proved in an ecclesiastical court referred only to the personal estate, not the real estate. Real estate belonged in theory to the King, from whom his subjects held, usually through a lower lord. Therefore, the disposal of it (technically the *will*) was effected through the royal or manor courts. Personal estate came from God, so it could properly be dealt with by God's representative, the bishop. This meant that the disposal of personal estate (technically the *testament*) covered a very minor part of the testator's property, if he held land.

Real estate consisted of houses, barns, shops, mills, etc, and any sort of land and associated rights connected with it held freehold or copyhold. Land under tenancy 'by Copy of Court Roll' was held from the manor, but descended automatically from father to son, failing whom, daughters, nephew, cousins who were descended from the original grantees. It was therefore a permanent holding for practical purposes.

Personal estate consisted of household furniture and bedding, pots and pans, clothing, farm stock and equipment, tools and stock in trade, crops growing and gathered, horses, carriages, wine, food, fuel, cash in hand, debts owing, securities for money lent to others – in fact, any perishable asset. Leasehold houses and lands were included, because a lease was temporary, even a long one.

Even quite important yeomen managed with very few personal possessions. Their houses were barely furnished, their clothing limited and their need for actual cash was not great, because of the great amount of barter trading. A will made at harvest time might show large amounts of crops and cattle, whereas one made in spring would find the barns empty. The personal estate could therefore be small, and the land holding considerable. As duty was payable to the bishop on the value of the estate declared, the wise testator naturally did his best to minimise this – our ancestors may not have been able to read and write, but they knew about tax avoidance schemes. Nonconformists were particularly adept.

Making the will

Henceforth the term 'will' is used to include both the will and testament as correctly used. Very few wills were made until the prospective testator was really aged (over 70) or in poor health. This was partly a reluctance to tempt fortune, or prospective heirs, into hastening the process; partly to retain the power of choice to the end; and partly because making a will cost effort, time and money, and no one wanted to do it twice. If a man in middle age, with a wife and family of eight, made a will, he could be reasonably sure that within a decade, his wife might die, some of his children certainly would, others might be born, he might acquire more property, or lose some, and have to rethink the sums he had given as legacies. There was also the fact that a will was a highly personal document, possibly the only chance an illiterate man had in his lifetime to express his views and opinions of his nearest and dearest. It was publicly declared, or at least to the witnesses, so a prudent man saved up his opinions until he was on his deathbed, and out of reach of retaliation.

A man who became at all ill knew that his time had come, with the primitive state of medicine then, and either wrote his will, if he knew how, or asked a friend, the parson or, later on, a lawyer, to do it for him. The practice would be for the writer to take down the provisions of the will from dictation, to go away and write it out, then come back next day and read it to the testator before witnesses. They were to attest that he was in his right mind and that he had listened to and accepted the will as correct. Then the testator and the witnesses signed or made their marks, in each others' presence. The witnesses could be, and usually were, beneficiaries under the will, who would naturally be at the deathbed.

Sometimes the process was left just too late. If the writer was slow, or the testator imminently dying, a *nuncupative* will could legally be made, in the presence of four persons. Provided the man stated what he wanted done and was sane at the time, the will could be written down afterwards and was valid though he died before signing it, as long as the witnesses agreed what he said. There is often a great deal of circumstantial detail about how he died and why there was no time to write down the will in the usual way.

What the will contains

A will normally starts with a religious preamble. Before 1700, this might read: 'In the Name of God Amen I Thomas Fludde of Little Notley in the county of X being sicke and weake in bodye but thanks be to God of goode and perfect rememberance do constitute and make this my last will and testament in manner and forme followinge that is to say first I bequeathe my sowle unto Almightye God my saviour and redeemer and my body to the earth from whence it came to be buryed at the discresion of mine executor hereinafter named and touchinge those worldly goods with which it hath pleased God to bless me . . .'.

This does not mean that the ancestor was particularly religious. The court was ecclesiastical, so the phrases were too. There might be an element of hedging bets by a man on his death-bed, but the grudging bequest of a few pence for 'tithes forgot' and sums for the upkeep of the bells and the altar, in early wills, often covers a lifetime of battling with the Church over those tithes. The fulsome religious phrases were mostly toned down in the secular 18th century, but are sometimes found in total as late as 1820.

Charitable bequests sometimes come next, varying from a few shillings to the local poor on the day of the funeral (sometimes distributed as beer and bread to the poor who carried the coffin), to regular doles on the anniversary of the death (the 'year's minde') or in perpetuity. If the last, there should be local records of administration as a charity. The direction to bury the body matters, if it is in the church, rather than churchyard (shows wealth or standing) or in a parish other than that of residence (?place of origin).

The next provision is usually that for the wife, which varies according to income, but is basically for house-room and income. If she is referred to as 'my now wife', there have been others. Conventional provision would be a small house or specified rooms in the family home, or just 'room and board' with the eldest son for life. If she is a step-mother, the terms of the legacy are likely to be very clearly set out, with precise rooms, rights, goods and services to which she is entitled. A widow is likely to be left an annuity, chargeable on the profits arising from the family business, or from the various family properties, often shared between a number of sons, each paying a small sum to her quarterly.

Sometimes, this financial legacy, possibly with a lump sum added, is said to be 'in lieu of her thirds' (or of widows' bench or dower). Strictly, a widow was entitled to a third of the real estate for life, which could be inconvenient if an adult son wished to run a farm or business as a unit. If the children were small, a widow might be left the main estate until they were adult, or even for life. A more usual provision is to limit this by adding 'if she remain my widow'. If she married again, she would lose house-room and all or most of her legacy. This was partly male chauvinist piggery, but partly an attempt to safeguard the interests of the children, for a new husband would take possession of all that she owned on marriage. A widow might be left household goods, or a share of them for life only or 'absolutely' or 'at her own dispose', which meant that she could sell or bequeath them in her turn. A wealthy man might even leave her a house and land for herself.

If no provision at all is made in the will for house-room for the widow, this has almost certainly been otherwise catered for by a marriage settlement earlier. A widow could not simply be thrown out when her husband died, even where relations were not good. She would have legal redress, which would be expensive, but would impoverish the family estate as well, so few men would risk it.

In the Name of God Amen I William Leech of
Wootton in the County of Oxon Labourer being in
health of body and of sound and disposing Mind and
Understanding praised be God, do make this my
last Will and Testam.t in manner following, and first
I will that all my just debts and funeral Expences
be paid and discharged. Item. I give and devise All
That my Messuage or Tenement with the Garden and
all and Singular other the p.mises thereunto belonging
Scituate and being in Wootton aforesaid wherein I now
dwell (after my wifes decease) unto my daughter
Sarah and her heires for ever. Item I give unto my
Son Thomas One Shilling. Item I give the use of all
my houshold goods unto my loving wife for the terme of
her life and after her decease I give the Said houshold
goods unto my Said daughter. Item I give all the rest
of my Estate unto my loving wife Elizabeth and her
Assignes and do hereby make my Said wife my sole
Executrix. In Witness whereof I have hereunto Set my
hand and Seale the Ninth day of June in the fourth
Year of the Reigne of King George the Second and in
the Year of Our Lord 1731

Signed Sealed Published and Declared by
the Said William Leech the Testator as   William Leech
and for his last Will and Testament   his
in the p.sence of us, and then Subscribed   ly Mark
by us as Witnesses at his request and in
his p.sence   Edw.d Hyves
                    Mary Gowler
                    John Bonn

Next comes the provision for the children. Normally, the eldest son would inherit the major part of the real estate. In the case of copyhold, this was automatic, and no mention would necessarily be made in the will. Most freeholds were likely to be 'limited' when purchased, to the man and his 'heirs', which meant first the eldest son. If these conditions are met, then the will may appear to leave nothing to this son, but to charge him with the payment of money legacies to his younger brothers and sisters. If the son is appointed executor, it is probable that he does inherit the main real estate even if this is not stated.

Younger sons may be given a secondary real estate, if this is available, in which case it must be stated. Otherwise, they are generally given a sum to apprentice them, or to set them up in business. The payment may be at 21, the standard age for receiving legacies, or postponed for some years, so that a heavy demand for cash does not cripple the family estate.

Daughters are generally given a money dowry, at 21 or a prior marriage with the consent of their guardian. Only if the father has a great deal of land is he likely to give this to a daughter. An eldest daughter occasionally gets more than the others. Daughters unmarried at their father's death were expected to live with their mother, or eldest brother, till they married. Sometimes a father would provide a cottage or annuity for a middle-aged daughter expected to remain a spinster.

Because a husband took his wife's property, a father who was suspicious of his son-in-law might leave a legacy to someone else on behalf of his daughter, to be advanced 'at his discretion as best he can arrange' and only paid to the girl if she became a widow. She might be given a life interest only, with remainder to her children after her death. Sometimes this was done to give the family an income they could rely on, if the husband was in debt, for sums paid wholly to her would be seized by his creditors.

Left: A typical 18th century will, that made by William Leech of Wootton, Oxon., in 1731. That he was a labourer shows that all classes may leave wills. Note his wife's life interest in the family home and the token shilling legacy to his son. The will was proved (below) five years later in the Court of the Archdeacon of Oxford (reproduced by permission of the Oxfordshire County Record Office, ref. MS Wills Oxon 140/1/15).

Occasionally, a wealthy man may leave certain of his children twelve pence (or other token sum) only. This is often referred to as '*cutting off with a shilling*' and regarded as proof of ill feeling. However, it often means that the adult son or daughter has already had his portion or her dowry from the estate. It is usually totally clear when the testator dislikes one of his children, because he says so. 'To my son John, twelve pence of current money, if he come and demand it, since he has been ungrateful and ill conditioned to his mother and myself these many years.'

Because these wills were made for illiterates and hand-copied by clerks, it was wise to include the names of all the children, even if they were to be 'cut off', since otherwise it was open for the aggrieved son to claim that his name had been omitted in the copying. The remark above makes Father's feelings quite clear.

If a man died leaving young children, or left a legacy to infant grandchildren, he would, if he were prudent, allow for at least some of them to die before the legacy was paid, usually at the legal age of majority, 21, or at such other age as the testator appointed. A daughter, in particular, might marry under age and die leaving issue, in which case he could allow the child or children to inherit what the mother would have received. He could order that the share of a child who died should go to the survivors of that group (*benefit of survivorship*), to another person, or back to the estate. If it reverted to the estate, it formed part of the *residue*.

Real estate would normally go to 'the eldest son and his heirs (or heirs male) forever', but a father determined to keep it in the family might *entail* it, by leaving it to the heirs *of the body* of the eldest son, then the second son, and his heirs of the body, and so on. It was often limited to the heirs male of the body of each son in turn, then to the eldest son of a named brother and his heirs male and so on (tail male). Only if the male heirs failed were the females let in, as heirs general, or right heirs. This is the way peerages descend mostly. If you find an entailed property in the family from way back, to which you appear to be entitled, forget it. Entails were broken in the 19th century and property cannot be left to generations far distant in the future. The only limitation which can be made is to living persons and those born within 21 years of the testator's death. 'Perpetuities' for land or money therefore failed.

However, attempts to establish an entail can lead to a very fine list of family names, all given with their relationships, often expressed as 'my nephew John son of my late brother William' and so on. The process whereby X will inherit if Y dies childless is called a *remainder* and can be written down briefly as 'If X dsp rem. to Y' or, for male descent, 'If X dspm, rem. to Y'.

If the will refers to 'surrendering (land) to the uses of my will' it means that the property is copyhold, held from some manor, often named. An estate left to persons as *joint tenants* is owned by them, not as tenants in the modern sense, and the survivor takes all. If they hold as *tenants in common*, they are also owners and their heirs will inherit the individual shares.

Married women could not make a will leaving property, even if they were heiresses. On marriage, their husband took the lot and could do as he wished with it – even the clothes in which they stood up could be given away. Even if real estate was left to her and her children after her death, the husband could claim a life interest, which was difficult to prevent. He would be owner as guardian of children under 21 anyway. Towards the end of the period, some advanced fathers left property to their daughters which they specified she could bequeath 'by will or deed in writing'. This deed needed the cooperation of the husband, could only deal with the property or money named, and it was a tough lady who dared to leave it other than to her husband or their children.

Widows and maiden aunts could and did make wills, and very often these are excellent value from the genealogical point of view, leaving small legacies and trinkets to every member of a large clan by name and description. If no will is to be found for a lady who obviously lived in affluent circumstances, it may be that she had a life interest only in all she possessed, which was then remaindered to another member of the family, under the will of husband or father.

Many wills contained bequests of 'mourning rings' to a large number of relatives and friends. Portrait lockets were also popular and, at the end of the period, brooches or lockets containing the hair of the deceased or a dead child. Silver spoons were passed down the family from generation to generation, and might be engraved with family initials. In many wills, the testator's clothing was divided among family and servants. A richly embroidered gown was a valuable gift and even everyday wear had a lot of use in it still, so these were legacies worth having. It is possible to sketch a picture of what a person wore from some wills.

The will should finish with a bequest of the residue of the estate, expressed as 'all other my goods and chattels, moveable and immoveable'. This covers everything not specifically bequeathed, including assets acquired after the will was made, if there is time. If no bequest of residue was made, then this should technically have been treated as if the person died intestate. In practice, the executor would probably take it. If a legatee died before the testator, or before getting the legacy, then this money would also fall into the residue if not otherwise directed. This rarely happened, since testators normally did a remainder.

An *executor* or executors were appointed – an *executrix* if female – who had to arrange the burial in a manner fitting the station of the deceased, pay and collect debts, prove the will – often done within a matter of days of the death – and arrange for the making of an inventory of the deceased's estate. Only after the full extent of the estate was established could he decide how much some of the legacies were worth. The will often directed that certain sums – for mourning or for the living expenses of the widow – should be paid immediately on death. Other legacies might be delayed for six or twelve months, to enable cash to be raised on an estate consisting of land or goods.

Legacies to minors were not due until the recipient was 21 or married, or some other age if the testator directed. Other bequests were postponed until after the death of the widow or another person with a life rent. Therefore the involvement of the executor with the estate might go on for years, and he

Even copyholds could be 'sold' for a nominal figure to a member of the family who was not heir at law. If it was done without agreement by the heir, there may be a dispute, but otherwise, the only record is in the manorial rolls. A son leaving to take up a trade in the town might have no interest in a small agricultural holding, and as long as he got a money portion, he was content.

Apart from these relatively formal methods, it is apparent that a great deal of property must have passed by informal gifts during life or on the deathbed, or was quietly removed by those who had charge of the dying person, especially if the heir was absent. Many families tried to bypass the expense of the probate court in cases where there was a simple family set-up, and for every one who was caught, dozens must have escaped. This accounts for a lot of 'missing wills'.

Where to locate wills

At the change to civil courts in 1858, probate records from many of the old ecclesiastical registries were centralised at Somerset House. In the 1950s/60s this process was reversed, and the records from the local courts were all redistributed to the appropriate diocesan record offices. In England these are normally the County Record Offices, with the following major exceptions:

Cambridgeshire: Cambridge University Library;
Derbyshire, Staffordshire, part of Shropshire: Lichfield J.R.O.;
Durham and Northumberland: University of Durham;
Rutland: Northamptonshire Record Office;
Surrey: Greater London Record Office;
Yorkshire: mainly at the Borthwick Institute, York.

Records for *London and Middlesex* are mainly split between Guildhall Library and the GLRO; some for *Shropshire* are at Hereford or the National Library of Wales; for *Warwickshire* are split between Lichfield and Worcester; and for *Westmorland* are split between Cumbria RO, Carlisle and Lancashire RO, Preston. Those for *Wales and Monmouthshire* are at the National Library of Wales, Aberystwyth.

There are, however, plenty of anomalies, where dioceses have not been coterminous with counties and where peculiars have included parishes in more than one county. The key to the various courts, their geographical coverage, and the present location, extent of and indexes to their records is J.S.W. Gibson's *A Simplified Guide to Probate Jurisdictions.* Two earlier books, published in 1974, and thus now rather out of date, may be found in libraries. These are Gibson's *Wills and Where to Find them* and *Wills and Their Whereabouts* by A. J. Camp, with very detailed information about the types of records. A summary by county of the location of wills, indexes and copies appears at the end of the complete *Wills Before 1858* (McLaughlin).

In these books lists of the parishes which belonged to peculiar jurisdictions or outlying parts of dioceses are given. Full addresses and locations of the various repositories can be found in *Record Offices:*

How to Find Them (Gibson), the *Record Office Guide* (Cole & Armstrong, FTM) and *Record Offices and Repositories* (Public Record Office).

Many indexes to these wills, and other records, have been printed and many more card-indexed in the repository concerned. Those without modern indexes should have semi-contemporary manuscript indexes, some made annually, some for blocks of years. They may be calendars – that is, a list of wills grouped by the first letter of the surname, not in absolute alphabetical order.

Copying wills and abstracting information

If you know the precise date of death of an ancestor, you can either use the index personally, or ask the record office concerned to check and send a photocopy of the will to you. They will normally do this if given exact information, but cannot undertake long searches in the indexes – especially in calendars – for someone undated, or for 'everyone called Bloggs'. They also cannot take time to make an abstract of the will for you, but may be able to recommend a searcher. Make sure that the searcher can really cope with the old writing and understands what the will means – there are far too many inexpert people in the trade now. Unless you know a reliable person, send for a photostat and transcribe at your leisure.

If at all possible, make an *abstract* of the will yourself. An example of reducing a page to a few lines is given in my *First Steps in Family History*. For help with reading the writing see the chapter on Handwriting.

Basically, you should note:

The name of the testator;

The place where he lived and his occupation if stated;

Special directions for burial;

The names of all legatees and the full details of the legacies;

Whether they were given for life only, for widowhood only, at a specified age;

What happens to the legacy if the first named person died;

Any odd clauses or personal comments on relatives;

The precise date when the will was made, and the probate date;

The names of executor(s), overseers and witnesses.

Although the dates are usually very close together, a sick person might recover, an old person last longer than expected. Legatees and executors may have died in the intervening period. The probate declaration immediately follows the will in the register copy, or is written on the back of an original will. If only one named executor proved the will, note if he is called 'surviving executor' or if 'power is reserved' to the other(s). Before the 18th century, this declaration will probably be in Latin. It should still be easy to pick out the name of the person proving the will, with some such descriptive word(s) as 'relict' (the widow) or 'filius' (son) amongst the legal verbiage – the other name will be that of the judge or court official before whom it was proved.

Inventories may be with the wills, or separately kept in the same office, or missing. Always ask. Administrations (*admons.*) may also be separated. They give limited information – normally only the name of the next of kin and his/ her relationship to the deceased, unless guardians have to be appointed for minors. There are occasionally other documents connected with probate, some of which, accounts for instance, can be quite informative. Definitions of these are given in the Glossary in *A Simplified Guide to Probate Jurisdictions*.

PCC Wills

The richer folk, who might have property in more than one diocese, tended to have wills proved in the Prerogative Court of Canterbury. So did those who wished it to be thought the family had, or those whose executors fancied a trip to London (though business could be done locally too), or were nonconformists who sought to avoid the local church dignitaries. Use of this 'top' court was far more widespread through the social spectrum than is generally realised, and a search for wills should always include PCC. For instance, towards the end of the period, the Bank of England would only accept probate from PCC. These wills are now kept at the Public Record Office and are accessible on film (see below).

Wills of soldiers and sailors, of those with property abroad, or who died in 'parts beyond the seas', also had to be proved in PCC. From 1654 to 1660, the bishops were no longer allowed to act as probate officials, and all wills had officially to be proved in London, at a civil registry, though many possessors of small estates managed to avoid this by making alternative arrangements or not bothering to prove unless someone informed on them.

Anyone can consult the PCC wills at the Family Records Centre in Myddelton St, Islington. You do not need to book or have a readers ticket. It speeds things up to have checked references first, since the queue for indexes can be long.

Alphabetical indexes up to 1699 have been printed and are available as hard bound books or on microfiche in large reference libraries or archives. The 1700–49 period has been indexed and is becoming available on microfiche in the same locations. The 1750 to 1800 period is printed and available in limp-bound white books. The period from 1801–25 is in process of being surname indexed and will be available in a year or two.

The 1826–53 period is calendered only, meaning all the wills of those whose names begin with A or B and so on are listed together annually in order in which the will was proved. The administrations follow the wills for that year.

In most of these indexes, county names only are given or 'Pts' (i.e. Foreign Parts) for those living or dying abroad, who had to use the Prerogative Court if they had any property in England or Wales too. This makes it quite difficult to trace a person with a common surname who died in London. There may be several 'John Brown, Middx' entries in a year.

From 1796, there is an alternative, in the Death Duty Registers (at the FRC), which from 1812 also index the 'Country Courts', thus providing a partially consolidated index for the whole country. Their use is far from simple and it is explained in *The Records of the PCC and Death Duty Registers* (J Cox) and briefly in the complete *Wills Before 1858* (McLaughlin).

For the final years 1853 to 1857, there is a printed index, attached to all sets on microfiche of the National Probate Indexes to modern wills, available in many Record Offices and libraries. The information is less detailed than after 1858.

To locate a will at the Family Records Centre, you must first find the reference (or quire number) in the calendars for that year or in the consolidated printed indexes. Old historical books may give you a reference for a will proved in a certain year by the name of its book (e.g. 14 ???Partridge), which is taken from that of a prominent testator whose will occurs early in that year. There is a simple key index to these old names which 'translates' them to a year.

In a second index book, find the stated year, and the group which includes your quire number in that year. Against it is the number of the film which has your will in it. When you have the film on the machine, roll through, looking at the top right hand corner of the frames, till you come to a page with your quire number (say 71) written large in the corner. The will you want, with the surname in the margin, could be anywhere in the next 16 pages; if you get to page 72, wind back very carefully, since the start of the will you need may be lurking at the bottom of the page. When you have found the will you need, make a careful note of the tiny individual page number, to make it easier to track down again.

You can make a copy personally for 10p an A4 page, or 25p if the staff do it. They have now withdrawn the paid search service whereby they would handle postal applications with the reference data. The Public Record Office, Kew, will also print copies at 35p from their own sets of wills, but it costs a minimum £10 for them to locate a will, even from the reference, and long wills may cost more than this. It is best to use a professional searcher if you cannot go yourself.

Inventories for PCC testators only survive from 1661 to the early years of the 18th century. There are modern indexes, partly published (see 'Inventories in the records of the PCC', by J.S.W. Gibson, the *Local Historian*, **14**, 4, November 1980).

PCY Wills

For northerners, the equivalent of PCC was the Prerogative Court of York (PCY), whose records are at the Borthwick Institute in York. The counties covered were Cheshire, Cumberland, Durham, the southern detachment of Flintshire, Lancashire, Northumberland, Nottinghamshire, Westmorland and

Yorkshire (also the Isle of Man). Indexes have been published to 1688, a modern consolidated index for 1688–1731 exists, with calendars as for PCC for the remainder of the period (both on microfilm at the Society of Genealogists).

Devon and Somerset

Wills for these counties were mostly destroyed at Exeter during the Second World War. Copies from the Estate Duty Office have been handed over to the respective County Record Offices, but they are incomplete and mostly date only from 1800. Many abstracts of Devon wills were made by Miss Moger before the loss, and some wills of Somerset gentry and connected families by Crisp. A great effort has recently been made by the record offices in both counties to collect copies of wills in private hands, from manorial records or quoted in land transfers.

Scotland

Probate was taken out of the Church's hands in 1560, but the new Commissariot Courts covered diocesan areas. Edinburgh was the over-riding court. All wills before 1823 are at the Scottish Record Office, General Register House, Edinburgh EH1 3YY. Most wills after 1823 are too, but others are at various sheriff courts (see *A Simplified Guide to Probate Jurisdictions*). Indexes to all courts to 1800 have been published by the Scottish Record Society.

Ireland

Here the vast majority of wills were destroyed with other Irish records in 1922, but determined efforts have been made to collect every remaining copy in private hands. The National Archives (Fourt Courts, Dublin) and the PRO Northern Ireland (Balmoral Avenue, Belfast, N.I.) have printed lists of what they hold, including numerous abstracts made by genealogists in the past. The Belfast Office also has Estate Duty Office copies of wills from 1821 to 1857. Irish residents (and Scottish, for that matter) with any property in England had their wills 'resealed' in London, and copies will be found among PCC wills.

Abstracts made by the antiquary, Sir William Betham, from wills proved in the Prerogative Court of Armagh (PCC equivalent) are fairly complete and are at PRO Dublin (microfilm copy at the Society of Genealogists). Other large collections of abstracts are held by the Church of Ireland Library (Church House, Church Avenue, Rathmines, Dublin 6), both Record Offices and the Society of Friends (6 Eustace Street, Dublin).

Glossary of terms

Many terms are explained in the text, but here is some of the jargon.

Administrator: man appointed by court to handle estate of intestate, or if no executor named in will, or if executor is under 21 or dead, mad or abroad.

At her own dispose, absolutely: she may sell, give away or leave by will.

Bond: promise to carry out will and produce inventory or pay named sum, twice value of estate as estimated.

Brother: often = stepbrother or brother-in-law.

Children: legitimate children only, unless clearly stated.

Copyhold: perpetual tenancy under lord of manor. Can be sold or bequeathed but normally passes to eldest son. Reverts to lord on intestacy with no male heirs.

Cousin: any relative other than brother, uncle, parent, etc. Often = nephew or niece.

Cousin german: first cousin.

Couverture: state of being married (for women only), without independent powers.

Dower: widow's entitlement to estate.

Dowry: sum given to daughter on marriage.

Executor/Executrix: man/woman appointed by testator to carry out provisions of will.

Father-in-law: often stepfather.

Fee simple: freehold, can be sold, not entailed or subject to reversions.

Fee tail, entail (tail male): freehold held for life with reversion to named heirs (male).

Free bench: widow's share of copyhold estate.

Heirs of the body: legitimate children.

Heirs male: sons, grandsons, or other males.

Heir: anyone inheriting or due to inherit property, by will or remainder.

Heirs general, right heirs: male or female heirs able to inherit under common law.

Heirs and assigns: heirs or persons given rights over property (eg, under mortgage).

Intestacy: dying leaving property but no will.

Issue: children.

Jointure: provision made by will or settlement for wife/widow by husband.

Messuage: large house.

Mother: may mean stepmother.

My terme (of yeares): the (rest of my) lease of property (unexpired).

Of the half blood: with one parent in common.

Own brother: one sharing the same father and mother.

Partial intestacy: incomplete will.

Probate: acceptance of a will as legally made by testator (before disposal of assets).

Put into hotchpot: include money advanced before death to a child in share-out.

Relict: widow of the deceased.

Remainder, reversion: legacy which takes effect after some other event (eg, death of the previous holder of property) or in certain circumstances (failure to pay money).

Tenant: holder, not usually person paying rent.

Tenement: holding, residence (not flat).

Testator/testatrix: man or woman making will.

Thirds: widow's share of whole estate

When he comes of age: reaches 21 or other age at which legacy is payable.

Reading a Latin will probate

Precise phrasing varies from place to place, and words are often greatly abbreviated. It looks a fearsome sight, but you only need three, or even two, things – the name of the deceased, the date when it was proved, and the name(s) of the executor(s). The rest is normally a piece of legal gobbledy-gook.

The name of the deceased may appear on line 1 or 2, eg

Rici Jarvis nuper de Haddenham Archinat. Buck. = Richard Jarvis
    late of Haddenham in the Archdeaconry of Bucks.

In the example shown opposite, we omit the name and go straight into:

Probat(um) erat hoc T(estame)ntum apud Oxon. = Proved was this
    Testament (will) at Oxford.

Then comes the date, '*decimo septo die mens(i)s Septembr(is) 1665*', the 16th day of September 1665. The year may be written in Latin first but is normally repeated in figures here or on the back of the will.

The next section is to the greater glorification of the official proving the will and can be ignored – unless, of course, you are related to the 'venerable man, Henry Alworth, doctor of laws and surrogate for Sir Giles Sweit, LL.D., officer of the Archdeaconry of Oxford'.

Look next for the name of the executor, more usually two to three lines from the bottom. Here the description is very much cut down as:

Petri Franckling fil(io) &c et un(o) Execut(orum) &c = Peter
    Franckling son *etc* and one Executor.

The '*&c*' would normally be expanded to:

filio naturale et legitimo = (to the) natural and lawful son;

and

uno Executorum in hoc testamento nominato = (to) one of the
    Executors nominated in this will.

Then come the standard probate clauses:

Cui com(m)issa fuit et est Ad(ministra)c(i)o(nem) [*Adco.*]
    om(niu)m et singulor(um) bonor(um) &c = to whom was
    committed administration of all and every of the goods;
d(ic)to def(unc)ti et ei(u)s T(estame)ntum = of the said
    deceased and his will;
qualiscumque concernen(tum) = (of) whatsoever it may concern;
in forma Juris Jurato Salve jure cuiuscu(m)que = in form of
    law sworn by oath with whomsoever (concerning to deal) justly.

If '*affirmato*' or '*affirmavit*' appears instead of '*jurato*', then you have a Quaker as executor.

Unusually, it was witnessed:

in p(rese)ntia mei Nic: Horsman, Reg(ist)rarii.

This is where the ordinary probate entry finishes. The names of the executors should match exactly what is in the (English) body of the will. Other forms of words often met with are:

Probate of the will of Giles Franckling of New Woodstock,· Oxon., 1665
(Oxfordshire Record Office, MSS. Wills Oxon. 1272/11, reproduced by kind permission)

> *unico executore/unica executrice* = (by) the sole (male) executor/
> (female) executrix;
> *relicta defuncti [rlca dfti]* = (by) the relict, widow of the
> deceased.

If the names don't completely match look for

> *executore subsisto* = the surviving executor;

or '*reservata*' or '*potestate reservata*' – power reserved – as in this case:

> *et reservata Elizabetha Franckling Ex(ecu)trici in hoc*
> *T(estame)nto etiam no(m)i(n)at* = and power reserved to
> Elizabeth Franckling in this will also (as) Executrix nominated.

Notice the curvy line over '*nominat.*' which shows that '*n*' or '*m*', or in this case both, have been omitted.

This may be followed by a further grant, often much abbreviated, but in this case written out in full, to the other executor. The second probate entry is dated 17th February 1665 – which is five months later, modern 1666, and before Nicholas Vilett, LL.B. The will is proved in much the same words by Elizabeth:

> *ux(or)is et alterius Execut' in hoc T(estame)nto No(m)i(n)at* =
> the wife and other (of two) Executors named in the will.

She is sworn '*bene et fidel(ite)r*' – well and faithfully – to administer and (to see to):

> *de solvendi Debita &c et Legata &c* = the paying of Debts etc
> and Legacies etc.

Her oath is taken in the presence of Jo(hn) Rhodes, '*No. Pubco.*', Notary Public.

If the named executor(s) die before taking administration, their own executors may do so. If the executor dies intestate, then the next of kin is granted administration. If the next of kin is under 21, then the next adult acts, as, eg

> *AB patruus eius (gardianus) causa minoritate Johannis B*
> *filii dicti defuncti* = AB his uncle on his father's side
> (guardian) by reason of the minority of John B son of the
> said deceased.

Sometimes, not all of the legacies in the will are due until some years later, when the executor has died and administration will then be granted to the same person as above:

> *de bonis non* = for the goods not (distributed).

Administration follows a similar pattern if an executor is abroad or is insane:

> *non compos mentis* = not whole of mind.

If you see strange names and '*creditores*', then the deceased died in debt and probate was granted to the principal creditor(s). If you find any other reasonably short form of words added to the probate entry, then it is best to ask the archivist for help. It may be a rewording of one of the phrases above.

If the word '*sententia*' appears against the probate entry, then there was a dispute about the will, and, although this is well worth knowing about, it does need a full command of Latin grammar and law too, so that you will need expert help, and probably more time than the archivist can spare. You may be able to pick out names and relationships. Get a photocopy, if possible, and submit it to a Latin expert.

LOCAL NEWSPAPERS

Back to the Bloggs

You check the will indexes for Bloggs in both counties, finding one for John died 1837, leaving property to his wife, to the chapel, and reasonable bequests to all his Independent children, though William and one of the sisters only got a shilling. However, young John, William's son, then aged 21 and recently married to Sarah Allan, was left £50, 'in the hope that he may walk with the Lord'. His sister Ann, married to Amos Griffin, a chapel member, got £50 too.

James, the second son of John and Jane, died a childless widower in 1852, leaving ten acres of land in Sprotley to his dear nephew John, son of his brother William, with reversion to John's eldest surviving son, or failing that to his brother William, now in Her Majesty's Army. That was how John got the chance to become a grazier instead of a shepherd. And that's where William, born 1823, vanished to. I wonder if he was killed in the Crimea?

There is a will for William Bloggs of Newchurch, mason, brother of John the Deacon, mentioning his own four children, and his nephew John son of John, to whom he leaves enough stone to build a wall round the extended graveyard.

Further back, there are a couple of farmers in Heatherley, a 'masoner' and a blacksmith in Morton, an Oliver Blogg in 1710, in Oldchurch, and a Jeames Blogge or Blagge 'sometime clarke' in 1679. These you note and order photostats, so you can transcribe them slowly at home, since the writing looks very crabby. And you notice that there seem to be quite a number of Blagges as well. With an uncommon name, it makes sense to collect every reference to the name–and variant spellings also.

Turning aside from the Bloggs dynasty, you have a look at the Maynards. The family names used by James Allan and Mary Elizabeth were very up-market, and her father was an auctioneer. The marriage is a bit surprising for the period, though the lady was a bit long in the tooth and, judging by the photograph which cousin Elsie eventually turns up, no beauty. Maybe she 'flung her bonnet over the mill' and her family made the best of it, as her James was willing to fit in with their standards. William Devereux Maynard's only son died after breaking his neck at a point-to-point race in 1871, so the father divided his estate between his two daughters for life. Sophia Matilda was over 40 and unmarried, so he selected his grandson, William Maynard Bloggs as his eventual heir in 1878, on condition that he took Maynard as his only surname.

Didn't you spot Maynard's Farm on the old map? Presumably James Allan Bloggs lived here till his first wife died, then his eldest son took over. There is a J.C.W. Maynard, Maynard's Court (farmer), in the phone book – maybe he is descended from that eldest son.

There are Maynard wills in the CRO and PCC too. Here you are rapidly into a new financial level. Grandfather Maynard was a very big farmer; his eldest son became a clergyman, and was the father of the curate who married the young couple in 1865. The second was to have the farm, but died just before his father. The youngest son, William Devereux, therefore inherited the farm, as well as acting as auctioneer and valuer, and it came to his grandson.

The farmer, William Maynard, makes his brother in law, George Augustus Devereux, gent., his executor in 1834. The marriage licences reveal one for William and Sophia Charlotte Devereux in 1799, but the marriage did not take place locally. Finally, you run it to earth in the cathedral city. One of the witnesses signed just Clissold. Was this Lord Clissold, who employed the shot gamekeeper?

Newspaper background

There are several possibilities here that additional information may be found in local newspapers. The first task is to discover what newspapers circulated in the county at the appropriate date. There is a reasonably complete list of newspapers from 1750 to 1920, and where their files can be seen, in *Local Newspapers* (Gibson Guide). This lists libraries and other repositories which hold copies; the British Library Newspaper Library at Colindale, London also has sets. Some newspapers have files themselves at their head offices, but access must be arranged in advance.

Not every town or even every county had a newspaper before 1800, and those there were covered a wide area. They were small, one or two folded sheets, so only the nationally or locally important, the shocking or bizarre things were recorded. The main reason for starting a London newspaper was to put forward some political view, but sales were promoted by including stories, ideally scandals, of high life, failing which, low life crimes and amusing oddities. Provincials copied most of their news from the Londons, with a few local items added.

The ordinary doings of ordinary folk did not become worth mentioning until the size of papers increased and their distribution area decreased. Originally, only the rich and prominent bought papers; as education improved and costs lowered, a wider social audience was pulled in by including reports of their own small triumphs and events. This was not, in most areas, until late Victorian times.

Crime – the assizes or petty sessions – comes first, and then other events happening in different villages, in roughly alphabetical order. If nothing interesting occurred, the village is omitted. Even if your ancestors are not mentioned, reading what happens in a particular village helps with background. A cholera outbreak, hard weather, poor harvests, the building of a railway nearby, all made a difference to your ancestor's life and may account for deaths or migration. Females were not expected to read the papers, so comments and descriptions could be quite explicit and the laws of libel rarely inhibited them.

Local events other than interesting crimes will best be sought in local papers – there were, before this century, no 'nationals' circulating everywhere on the day of publication, so the locals reprinted snippets from London-published papers or other provincials. A major theft or a good juicy murder will be reported in all areas. The killing of a gamekeeper by poachers was fairly run of the mill, unless there were aggravated circumstances, but will certainly be reported locally, when it happened and when the men were caught, tried and hanged.

Of the later events, there is unlikely to be comment on the young soldier, William Bloggs, even if he died, unless he sent back a written report of one of the battles, with enough gore to please the readers. Nowadays, most local deaths are noted – then, only the more important people rated a mention. Mr Maynard the rich farmer, his son the auctioneer, and certainly the son and grandson who were clergymen, will have an obituary and funeral report. Most of the Bloggs family will pass without comment. William, the young shepherd, and his little son, buried by coroner's order, should have an inquest report. The month was February, and the obvious cause is being frozen to death while attempting to tend or rescue lambing sheep. They may not be named, but simply styled *'a shepherd of Sprotley and his lad'*. True, they may be squeezed off the page by a long report of what the local squire said in the House of Commons, or even *'Hunting spoiled by bad going in Dingley Bottom'*.

News of poor or ordinary persons only appears if they are doing something extraordinary. Crimes are well reported, and sudden deaths from natural causes may be if they happen in unusual circumstances (the husband who died of a heart attack beside his bed-ridden wife, who was too crippled to get assistance and therefore starved to death). Childbirth is not news, but three sets of twins followed by triplets is, especially if they mostly lived. Occasional 'social conscience' pieces were published in the two-sheet papers, with details of the sufferings of named paupers, through the workings of the Corn Laws, or the famine in the Hungry Forties. Agricultural contests give the names of champion ploughmen, or long serving housekeepers, or growers of prodigious marrows and turnips.

After about 1880, locals, especially newer ones seeking readership, include petty crimes and misdemeanours, fires, problems with drains and sewage, school attendance and vaccination cases, geographical lectures, Methodist musical evenings, Baptist bunfights, Sunday school outings, golden wedding interviews, holders of gun licences, farm wages, and obituaries and funerals. The Births, Marriages and Deaths column can be disappointing.

On Thursday last, to the wife of Mr A. Jones, a son.

But it may include distant events to members of local families who have migrated or emigrated, enabling you to follow all strands of kinsfolk.

Fuller details of how newspapers developed and what is likely to be found in them at different times is in my guide *Family History From Newspapers*.

The marriage of William Maynard, farmer, to what appears to be his social superior, in the presence of a peer, sounds like a good story. It may be reported locally, if there was a newspaper. If not – and 1799 is early for most papers – then try the *Gentleman's Magazine* (1731–1868), which has been indexed. It has the whiff of the sort of scandal the idle gentlemen who read it would enjoy. Most persons mentioned are gentry, of course;

Mr De Vere, son to Lord Stonybroke on Thursday last past married Miss Figgins, an heiress of 13,000L., at Bath Abbey.

However, there are often obituaries of craftsmen who served the rich; actresses; ancient soldiers; abnormally old, tall, fat, short persons; foreign eccentrics or freaks. Some material must have been contributed by local readers, interested in the oddity of their surroundings. The persons may be described by initials or occupation only, which is sufficient if you know roughly what you are looking for.

ANNALS OF THE POOR

The fault is great in man or woman,
Who steals a goose from off a common;
But what can plead that man's excuse
Who steals a common from a goose?
The Tickler Magazine, 1 Feb. 1821

Where did they come from?

At some point, you will be faced with having traced back ancestors in a parish register to the point where they run out. There are, for instance, no Bloggs entries in Peasley before 1761, when John and Sarah of that name commence to baptise. They were not married in the parish. Where did they come from? The obvious move here is to consult the local Marriage Index, in the hope that they wed in his or her place of origin.

If this leads you to a marriage in X, but there are no baptismal entries for groom or bride, you are no further back. Similarly, if your ancestor arrived out of the blue in a new place and married there 'of this parish', what can you do? First, consider his status. If he is well-to-do, then probably the best way to track him is to study wills, one of which, with luck, will say '*my son John Bloggs now of Peasley*'. But if he is poor, then a will reference is less likely (though never forget the bachelor uncle with a bit of spare cash). But what about the poor.

Too many people have been deterred from tracing their ancestors in the past by the fear that 'there won't be anything about them'. Others have been led to invent romantic tales because they think (a) they will never find the truth, (b) no one else will either. But it is rash to assume that poor ancestors left no documentary evidence behind them. In fact, the poorer they were, the more there is likely to be.

Back to 1837, everyone should be documented at St Catherine's House and/or in censuses. Before that, parish registers give details of poor as well as rich and there is just as likely to be a personal comment about the appearance, habits and character of a poor man as the Squire – perhaps more so, since he probably could not read and object.

The parish poor

Before 1834, the parish itself was the normal unit of local government, administered by a collection of untrained officials, chosen from among the local inhabitants and ratified by the local untrained magistrates. The most important were the two churchwardens, who saw to the upkeep of church and churchyard, parish cottages, charities, etc, and kept an eye on religious and moral welfare; and the two overseers, who looked after secular welfare in the parish, including highways, bridges, watercourses, and the poor people.

Each parish was responsible for its own poor. There were five basic classes of persons needing relief:

> the sick;
> the aged;
> widows, deserted wives and orphans;
> unemployed able-bodied inhabitants;
> destitute wanderers or temporary residents.

The sick were given nursing, not by trained nurses, but by village women with aptitude and/or time; possibly medicine; and in extreme cases, surgery, which tended to prove fatal equally for rich and poor. Most illnesses ended rapidly in recovery or death, but a few men survived damaged, living in the parish for years, maimed or handicapped. They were expected to do what they could to support themselves, but might be given a small allowance, have their rent paid, and get occasional hand-outs of bread and clothing from charity funds.

Widows who could do so were encouraged to support themselves, and were sometimes given spinning wheels and a stock of wool as a starter. Some did parish nursing or laundry work. Those with young children got allowances and rent, but were encouraged to marry again or take in actual orphans or the aged, for whom they were given allowances.

Orphans and widows' children were supported while small and their allowance paid to whoever cared for them. Like other village children, they had to do whatever work they could from about seven years old, helping about farms, watching livestock, etc. At about 14, they were apprenticed at the parish charge, sometimes to a craft, more often to 'husbandry' or 'domestic arts', meaning they were unpaid drudges in farms or houses. Normal apprenticeships ended at 21, but parish ones lasted until 24, giving the employer three more years of free service for the cost of their keep. Some masters paid a little in the last years, but it wasn't compulsory.

The aged were given an allowance, rent and nursing if need be, not at a set age, but when they could no longer work. Finally, they would be buried at the expense of the parish, which was not, at least in the country, necessarily a cheap and undignified ending. A pauper would, in a good parish, be decently coffined, borne and followed by mourners, encouraged by a dole of bread and beer from the parish. It was after 1834 that a 'pauper funeral' became such a bitter disgrace.

In some places there were almshouses (charity funded) which provided a comfortable last home for single or widowed aged. Applications state age and length of residence and maybe other details – though few survive now.

All these classes of paupers might be given extra doles of clothing from time to time, from the overseers or churchwardens via charities. Clothing was basic – shirts, shoes, shifts, the occasional waistcoat or coarse gown. A poor apprentice was started off with a kit of clothes, then his master had to provide more as the lad grew, as necessary.

Able-bodied men who could find no work for the time were found a task about the parish. Roads and bridges always needed repair and water-courses to be cleaned out. Later, men were sent round ratepayers, who were obliged to find work for them for a number of hours. Men could not work in a craft to which they had not been apprenticed, but farming, haulage and general carrying was anyone's meat. A craftsman fallen on evil times (by fire, say) might be lent money and expected to repay when he was on his feet again. Only in general unemployment would an able-bodied man get an allowance, though his wife and children might be relieved if he was doing his best to help himself. Rent might be paid while a man was unemployed, though if it looked likely to be long-term, he might be moved into a 'parish house' kept for the purpose.

All details of the various allowances paid and why, should be in the Overseers' Accounts for the parish, except for charitable grants which were the affair of the churchwardens. The Churchwardens' Accounts list work done on the church, churchyard and parish houses and may name craftsmen and their labourers. Not only wages but the amount spent on beer to wash down the plaster, etc, may be stated.

These account books were kept in the parish chest in the church when not in use, with apprenticeship indentures for poor children. Two copies were written of these on one sheet of parchment, cut across with a wavy or indented line. The master kept one, the parish the other, till the full term was served.

Where did the money come from?

The money to provide the various allowances and to pay for parish-financed works was then collected from the local inhabitants by the overseers, according to the assessed value of their property. The overseers had to calculate how much in total was likely to be needed, based on the previous years, but could call for a supplementary rate if sudden calamity occurred. If this was specific to one village, aid might be sought from other parishes by sending a letter to be read out in church. Collections 'for a Brief from So-and-so parish on account of the great Floode there' were made all over the country. Some personal losses through fire and flood were the subject of Briefs, and they are sometimes listed in the backs of parish registers. This was a charity collection, not a fixed sum.

Because the overseers were themselves ratepayers, they did not have the casual attitude to rate levies that modern paid officials may have. They spent no more than they had to, and sometimes pared down allowances to fit the money collected, rather than ask for more. Most parish overseers were just, if only because they knew that one day, they or their families might be a recipient, not a payer. It was reckoned fair to have the better-off members of the community pay to support men who had given good service to that community in their youth, or their widows and orphans. It was fair to help a man who was sick, or had a setback through misfortune. It was not at all fair to pay out good money to support someone who was too idle or too drunken to support himself. The overseers knew all their clients and could apportion blame or show compassion with due regard for natural justice rather than the letter of the law. An aggrieved pauper could appeal, but most justices took the word of the overseer.

It was regarded as totally unfair to have to support someone who didn't belong to the parish, but had come in and got into a situation which required relief. The stock of parish money was finite, and should go to parish folk. This was a very reasonable concept, which gave rise to a lot of misery in practice.

Settlement rules

In theory, each person had a 'place of settlement' where he belonged and was entitled to poor relief. It was simple enough for a man whose ancestors had always lived in the parish where he now resided. In time of trouble, the parish would cheerfully help – probably the overseer was some sort of relative. It was when someone moved from a home parish that problems arose. If there were no jobs or houses, if he had made himself locally unpopular, if he was ambitious, a young man might decide to move. If he settled down, worked hard and behaved himself, he would progress upwards in the community, probably serve a parish office and, in age or want, have earned himself the right to support from the new parish. If things went wrong, he and his family were in trouble.

Up to 1662, a man could re-establish settlement by living in a new parish for three years. He might come in by invitation as a labourer for a farmer or tradesman, or, daringly, arrive and offer his services. This was risky, because spare houses would not be available. He could, if he had the nerve, build a small habitation on the manor waste, as long as he could get it up and a fire going inside 24 hours. This needed co-operation, and implied he had friends and a job lined up already. Every house should have had four acres with it, so an undesirable could be evicted and his house pulled down on those grounds, if necessary.

The law was tightened up until, in 1687, a man could be thrown out within 40 days of arrival, unless he had a house worth £10 a year (a large property). From 1691, he couldn't sneak over the boundary and lie low for 40 days, but must give notice of arrival, which was read out in church and written in a book, then wait 40 days. Most parishes threw out newcomers on principle, in case they should become poor or, worse, die leaving widow and orphans to

The Examination of Benjamin Bishop of the Parish of Wendover in the County of Bucks Labourer concerning his place of legal settlement taken upon Oath before me C. Tumor, Clerk, one of his Majesty's Justices of the Peace in & for the said County this 29th day of Novr. 1813 —

Who saith, that he believes he was born in the Parish of Williston in the County of Bucks, & that when he was about thirteen years of age he was hired by the week to Mr Gore of Tring in the County of Herts. as a Ploughboy at 4/6 p week. & served him three years — He next hired himself to Mr Gregory in the Parish of Tring in the same County as a Servant in Husbandry for one year at the wages of 3.10.0 & at the expiration of that year, he hired himself again to the said Mr Gregory for another year at the wages of 4.0.0 — On leaving Mr Gregory's service, he hired himself to Mr Geary of Wendover in the County of Bucks for one year at 5.5.0 wages. After serving Mr Geary a year, he hired himself for a year to Mr Billington of Berkhamstead in the County of Herts, whom he served about 6 months, & was then drawn to serve in the Herts militia & served accordingly. After serving about three years in the Militia, he went to Sittingburn in the County of Kent as a day Labourer, where he remained about twelve months, & then enlisted into the 15th Regt of Light Dragoons at Sittingburn. He served in that Regt 7½ years, & was then discharged in consequence of his wounds, & was sent to Garrison duty in the Tower in London, where he served rather more than years, he was then discharged, & went again to day labor at Chelsea where he continued about 4 years; he then went to a haymaking about Enfield & returned to Wendover about six weeks since — This Examinant further saith, he does not know that he has done any act since he left the service of Mr. Geary in Wendover, whereby he has gained a Settlement elsewhere —

Sworn before me
C. Tumor, Clerk

the mark of ✝ Benjamin Bishop

An Examination as to Settlement, 1813.

the care of the parish. 'Here's a stranger, heave half a brick at him' was the rule, not a joke.

The normal ways in which a man could obtain or change his settlement were as follows:-

a. being born in a parish of a settled father;
b. paying taxes on a property in the parish;
c. serving as a parish officer (normally chosen from the ratepayers);
d. being apprenticed to a settled man for seven full years;
e. by being hired to work for a settled inhabitant for a complete year of 365 days.

The second and third implied money – and so less probability of needing relief. The fourth kind usually meant father had paid a premium. Some parishes aimed to apprentice their paupers – especially those from non-established families – outside the parish, to transfer the claim for future relief. A broken apprenticeship didn't count, so if the master died, that might be that, unless his relatives took over.

The last way was the common one by which a settlement was changed. Employers, as ratepayers, avoided casually adding to their own potential burden, by taking on men at one Hiring Fair and discharging them the day before the next. Until a man proved he was useful and healthy, he was never hired for the full year (actually a year and a day). It had to be continuous too – many a man had cause to regret asking a kind employer for a couple of days off for a family emergency. That broke his service.

Married men, especially those with children, were not allowed to resettle in this way. From 1697, they were permitted to come to a new village only if they could bring with them a Certificate of Settlement from their old parish, agreeing to take them back if they became chargeable to the rates. Tradesmen coming with a certificate could not bring their apprentices, who might thus become settled. 'Certificate men' only became settled when they started paying taxes or served a parish office.

If the non-settled man fell on evil times, he was sent back swiftly to his own parish. Certificate men were sent in a cart at the home parish's expense, which meant that most parishes would not issue a certificate for new homes over 20 miles or so away, over which removal costs became expensive. A man without a certificate might be dumped over the boundary to die in a ditch, especially if he was a wanderer from place unknown. For the ordinary labourer, the rule was that a Removal Order must first be obtained from a magistrate, and that this could be suspended if the person was sick. This rule was frequently broken.

A woman took her legal settlement from her husband, so if a man worked in a parish for years without gaining a settlement and married a local girl and died, his widow and children could be evicted from the only home they had ever known to a place where they were strangers. If the husband's family were not really local either and it just happened to be where he had once worked for 365 days, she wouldn't be very welcome. Some widows were set adrift to walk 'home' a few days after the husband's funeral.

Legally, a Removal Order had to be obtained, but these were often challenged, where the man's links with his parish of settlement were tenuous. Getting an order was complicated. First there was an 'Examination as to Settlement' which may state a man's birthplace and parentage and his career to when he arrived in the parish, with names of employers, wages and duration of service. The better the claim, the less detail. To avoid complications after a death, the overseers tended to examine anyone who looked like becoming chargeable – a bad cold aroused suspicions. A really awkward case would be challenged by the 'home' parish which might adduce details of the father's and grandfather's settlement. Sometimes a parish paid out more in legal fees fighting a claim for settlement than it would have cost to keep a whole family for years.

The settlement parish could pay over the sum due for relief and leave the man or family where they were, if the new parish agreed. In this case, the payment out will be entered in the accounts of the home parish – a useful proof of connections over a distance.

Removal Orders and Examinations as to Settlement would also have been kept in the parish chest originally, and were carefully preserved lest the same man or family should try to re-enter the parish. To go through the legal process twice would have been very costly. Short details of the case will be found in the Quarter Sessions records, if the parishes fought about a settlement.

Bastards

Bastards were a special case, also dealt with extensively. See the chapter on Illegitimacy.

Where are they now?

All these papers from the parish chest may still be there, or may have been destroyed when no longer current, or given away as salvage in wartime. Some parchments were reused for bishop's transcripts if the backs were clean, or to stiffen book covers. Many have been deposited in County Record Offices and others trickle in still from time to time. Those still in churches, often in unlocked chests, are at risk from vandals or souvenir hunters.

Occasionally, an account book is in private hands, where the overseer served frequently and came to regard the book as his own. Descendants will sometimes deposit, if they are told what the old things are.

Even when the accounts are fragmentary or lost, a knowledge of the system will help to estimate what is probable. The settlement system was a brake on the mobility of labour among ordinary families and it restricted the range of movement. Craftsmen could move more easily and single men were more mobile than families.

The country labourer

The countryman had certain practical advantages over the towndweller. Even if his cottage lacked the legal four acres, he probably had a large garden, where he could grow vegetables and keep hens and a pig or two. Pre-enclosure, he also had certain rights over village common land, of grazing a cow, sheep, geese, etc, of collecting dead wood or turf where customary, and acorns and beechmast from the woods for his pigs, and the odd rabbit for the pot. Village women and children were allowed to glean or leaze – to gather up the fallen ears of corn after harvest – and the family could live well and even have a little surplus for sale in a good year.

Farm wages were fixed by the Justices, and fixed low, but only the beginner was restricted to these and he mostly lived in at the farm, so got food and keep. The householder was part self-supporting, part wage-earner – and these increased if he was any good. When the old open-field cultivation system ended, so did common rights. Enclosures allowed farmers to fence off blocks of land and asserted the right of the lord of the manor to all commons.

The cottagers lost common rights and therefore could not keep large animals. They were forced to rely more on wages, so the lowness mattered. Much free food was lost, for themselves and their animals, so was free wood for firing. Women gleaning were accused of theft, since the farmers wanted to fatten their own hogs on the corn fallen. More and more men who had been part-time workers now competed for jobs. In enclosed villages, distress was great by the 1790s and men fled to still-open villages, placing a great strain on them. There was a war on, and prices were rising rapidly, so even the wealthy noticed the desperate poverty to which farm labourers had fallen. Philanthropists tried to do something about it and even officials like magistrates decided that something should be done, if only to safeguard themselves from a Revolution, like the one across the Channel.

The Speenhamland System

In 1795, a group of magistrates met in an inn parlour at Speenhamland, Berkshire, with the declared aim of fixing higher wages. Several drinks later, they ended by suggesting a rise plus free potatoes and fuel, but fixing merely the minimum rate at which parish allowances were paid. This was to reflect the price of a gallon loaf. A man could have the equivalent of three loaves a week, women and children one and a half each. This minimum was speedily adopted as a maximum, instead of any wage increase, and was later pared down.

Each parish had its own system for coping with the able-bodied poor. Some collected more money or set them on parish work, but numbers increased with new enclosures. Most settled for the new 'roundsman' system. A poor unemployed man had to go round the local tradesmen and farmers till he found one to offer work. Ratepayers had to employ them – which pressed heavily on the craftsman who could not use unskilled labour and the small farmer, managing with the help of his sons, who could not afford outside labour. Some of these were ruined and joined the ranks of the poor.

The large farmers liked the idea, because they paid half wages and the parish the rest, making it up to Speenhamland levels. Some farmers dismissed their regular workers and used roundsmen only. A really cunning man employed men from the next village, so he didn't have to pay rates as a contribution.

The roundsman system was degrading, with workmen always begging for the chance to work. It increased the gap between rich and poor, but at least it kept men at home, and in work some of the time. In some places, old-established farmers tried to keep on their old workmen, and increased demand for produce during the Napoleonic Wars helped to absorb some extra labour.

Then the war ended and with it the artificial prosperity. Imports competed for markets and there was a series of bad harvests, partly caused by over-cropping in the days of high demand, and a failure to rest or fertilise the newly enclosed fields. The old system may not have been efficient, but at least it allowed land to rest and running livestock on it helped to fertilise it naturally.

This ruined more farmers – often the better-natured ones, with long-established local connections and poor relatives among the workers. It let into the countryside a new class of 'money-men' – war-profiteers and City merchants, who bought up country estates and tried to run them like counting houses.

The moneymen slashed the Speenhamland allowances to the bone – to two loaves a week – and rejected the sensible suggestion of providing land allotments for the poor to rent to support themselves. They treated the grumblings caused by malnutrition and real distress as revolutionary infection from France. They also introduced machinery into farming, since it speeded work and needed no food. This increased unemployment and when desperate men burnt ricks, stole turnips and broke machinery, this was taken as proof of political sedition. As the money-men had become magistrates too (which went with owning the 'Big House') they were able to punish the poor savagely.

Crime

Increasingly, the records of the poor are the records of crime. A poor man had only to step a little out of line to be severely punished. Claiming old common rights resulted in punishment for gleaning (by criminal grannies) or picking up dead wood and beechmast. Snaring rabbits was worse than stealing turnips, since it spoilt the fun of gentlemen who wanted rough shooting. Organised demonstrations against machinery in 1830, called 'Captain Swing' riots, after their mythical leader, were savagely repressed, and 400 men were transported to Australia for life. Many men died in an attempt to poach rabbits or game, for the keepers set lethal spring guns on paths and in coppices. This did not count as murder, though attacking keepers did. The choice was often a straightforward one between starvation and crime. Many of the 'criminals' were only doing what their ancestors had done as of right, with the added incentive that they were now poaching to save their families from starvation. They felt they had more right to the wild produce than incoming strangers, even if these men had bought the manor house and park.

Apart from semi-political crimes – which would now come under the umbrella of legitimate trade union activity, the poor were inevitably more likely to figure in normal crime statistics. Although they were not necessarily more criminal than the rich, they had more reason to commit crimes and far more chance of being found out and punished. Court records of any period are worth checking for a reference to a poor ancestor. Indeed, the only ancestors who are easy to trace before parish registers – apart from property owners – are criminals. You may give thanks for coming of a long line of horse thieves.

At all stages from the 16th century, justice was dispensed locally by untrained magistrates (JPs) often sitting informally in their own houses, and by the King's judges, who travelled on circuit round the country. They visited county towns about four times a year, and the records are preserved in the Quarter Sessions rolls. They dealt with a ragbag of offences, from failure to repair roads and bridges by way of bastardy and settlement cases to murder and theft. Some rolls have been abstracted and printed, or unpublished calendars may be available in County Record Offices. See *Quarter Sessions Records* (McLaughlin).

A complete list, county by county, for England and Wales, of years covered and the extent of calendars and indexes, etc, is in the Gibson Guide to the whereabouts of *Quarter Sessions Records*.

The volumes are huge (or are still in actual rolls) and ease of reading varies according to period. The case will be referred to several times, from the indictment onwards. The jury may find a 'True Bill' or case to answer, in which case, it went to trial. The accused may be remanded on bond to appear later, or be kept in gaol. A bond had to be backed by two guarantors, often relatives or friends from the home village, which helps if the crime is committed elsewhere, since it is the location of the crime which is stated in the indictment. (The accused is usually described as of that place, as he had at least briefly been so at the time of the crime. If he was described as of somewhere else, and that could be shown to be wrong, then the case could fail.) The witnesses also had to swear bonds to appear and their guarantors may be useful also (for those who dislike the idea of finding their ancestors accused of crime, remember they may figure as the injured parties or as witnesses).

Some cases hang on from session to session and then fizzle out – probably because the accused had had lawyers or friends working behind the scenes on his behalf. Also in the days before a professional police force, prosecution of crime and administration of justice was haphazard and inefficient.

Both charges and sentences may seem peculiar to modern eyes. Stealing a handkerchief or a rusty horseshoe may be punished by transportation, whereas assault and battery on a tax collector rated a sixpenny fine. A great deal depended on the status and friendships of the accused and the personal inclinations of the judge that day. The lower courts are even less consistent. Theft of property worth more than 40 shillings was a hanging matter, which accounts for the merciful alteration of value to 39 shillings 11 pence. Personal vendettas and prejudice played a great part, so a poaching fine may be followed by window breaking at the informant's home, and an uppity labourer whose real crime was agitation for better wages may be framed on a charge of theft to get rid of him.

Letters by the judge or diaries of local gentry, or careful investigation done as a university thesis, may have since been published or deposited at the local CRO. This could show the reason for a really odd decision. Sometimes a bout of indigestion or a hangover may be the only cause of unusually severe punishment for a trivial crime.

The poor in the towns

Very large towns, of which there were few before 1850, were special cases in regard to settlements and the way in which they dealt with the poor. London, Sheffield, Birmingham, Manchester, Bristol and a few others were large enough to be anonymous. Men could go there on speculation, with a very good chance of finding a job within a day or two, provided they were adaptable and did not have ideas of setting up for themselves in a craft trade, in competition with the City fathers. The rule that only apprenticed men could trade in a craft was intensified in London to mean only locally apprenticed, though a fully qualified provincial could buy his way into a local trade guild or company if he had enough money and a friend at court. This was not open to a poor man, who had to depend on finding an employer.

Towns could absorb any number of strong young men (and even women). There was no place for the weak or sick or aged, however. A man could work till he died of industrial disease or the fevers which ravaged the mean streets. If he recovered but was too ill to work, he might try to stagger back 'home' or be sent there, for it was very difficult indeed to get a settlement in a town, and no certificates were issued to let the men move elsewhere. One alternative for able-bodied labourers who had failed in one town was to try another – so the main roads were thronged with travellers trying their luck.

The large towns, and even some smaller ones, were run by a Mayor and burgesses, not parish elders, though they called themselves 'the Vestry'. Little lip service was paid to the religious duty of succouring the poor and needy. It was something which had to be done, to keep untidy heaps of beggars and dying off the streets. There was little sense of community for all classes in the place. Many labourers were newcomers who had come seeking work and fortune and failed to make it. There were few really old local families among the poor – people got on or got out. Some of the employers operated a sort of benevolent scheme for their own men, but for most, the security net was full of holes.

Workhouses

Towns rarely gave out-relief (leaving paupers in their own houses and paying rent and allowances). They preferred to eject their poor and pack them into purpose-built workhouses, after 1722 (earlier in London). The system was to appoint a workhouse master and leave him to administer the poor. He had a certain amount to spend on food, so he aimed to keep down the number of paupers sharing it. He failed to provide nursing for the sick, turned pregnant girls out into the snow and kept the poor on such inadequate rations that they died fast of starvation. Because town workhouses took in not only the sick, mad and pregnant, but also able-bodied men and their families, an alternative name was the House of Industry. The poor had to earn their keep – or, precisely, to add to the profit. Stocks of wool, leather and metal, etc, were provided and the inmates were set on producing goods, sold for the profit of the master and vestry. Sometimes the workhouse did sub-contract work for local mills, sometimes the products were sent to rival towns to undercut prices there. At least this was better than picking oakum, a gaol punishment also used in some country workhouses to keep the able-bodied out of mischief.

Because extra paupers meant more useless mouths to feed, the master segregated males and females. If a girl came in pregnant, she and her infant stood a good chance of dying. Only if a girl caught the eye of the master was she likely to get pregnant after arrival. Division of the sexes broke up many hitherto happy families, for the men often deserted from the workhouse and ran off alone, leaving their families to suffer.

Some workhouses have surviving records listing inmates, which give date and place of birth, occupation, reason for entry plus career in the workhouse. Other books listed diet and clothing and possibly work done and profits – though the workhouse masters tended to play it close to the chest. Often these records were destroyed, since they gave away too much. If they exist, they should now be in county or town archives. Some of the worst cases of abuse were brought to public attention and investigated, in which case there may (at least in the 19th century) be a newspaper report.

The New Poor Law

In 1834, control of relief of the poor was taken away from the parish and transferred to the Union, which was a group of six, a dozen or more parishes, according to size. Control was in the hands of a Board of Guardians, chosen from local gentry, clergy and major tradesmen, in most cases not even remotely related to or familiar with the paupers they were asked to relieve. They were thus inclined to look after the interests of the ratepayers entirely, not the paupers. Poverty now was regarded very much as somehow the fault of the poor person – even somewhat of a crime, to be punished by harsh treatment. The Board could never imagine the day when their families or themselves would be paupers, so they did not mind establishing a precedent of harsh treatment. Workhouses had been spreading gradually to most medium-sized towns, especially those on main roads, and now every Union built at least one. Out-relief was almost abolished and some poor who would otherwise have been only temporary paupers, had their rent been paid for a few weeks, were forced to break up their homes and move into the 'House' or forego relief. The normal thing for a pauper, without relatives who could or would help, was the workhouse. Hard work and short commons were all that an aged labourer could look forward to, and the sheer disgrace of ending in the workhouse was enough to kill off many paupers rapidly.

The vestiges of the settlement system still operated and any poor who could be said to belong to someone else were sent back to their own Union workhouse as soon as the magistrates' order could be obtained. As certificates had been abolished, many poor persons had no sure 'home' Union, but might be shunted to and fro while legal wrangles continued. Relatives were not allowed to take in pauper children unless they could indemnify the parish, which only the better-off could do.

One of the added bitternesses attached to workhouse life was that most of the poor had to wear a sort of uniform, a coarse gown or cotton suit, sometimes with 'P' for pauper and a letter for the name of the parish. Their own clothing and any small possessions were taken from them on entrance. If they ran away from the intolerable House, they had stolen the uniform. The sexes were separated, and old couples of 50 years standing ended their days apart, enduring the last indignities among strangers.

Records of this period should also be found in county or town archives, but Minutes of the Board of Guardians tend to concern themselves with self-congratulations, not details of paupers. They are most useful when an attempt was made to force a distant relative to pay for pauper support, since the addresses of known relations are recorded, with their replies to the demands. This covers a period of general migration from country to town.

Rogues, vagabonds and sturdy beggars

Anathema to the parish authorities were the folk who wandered the country with no settlement or any wish for one and no visible means of support. They were lumped together as 'rogues, vagabonds and sturdy beggars' and it was permissible to eject them or throw them in the village lock-up, at will.

Naturally, some were wandering bands of thieves, ready to steal anything which wasn't nailed down and to con the locals out of food and money with hard luck stories. Some of the beggars painted on or self-inflicted wounds or ulcers, which they swore they got in the wars, though they mainly did their act in towns or at fairs, where the audience was large. There is little record of these men, since they rarely left cards.

Companies of actors and circus-type performers also travelled round the country in carts. The only early theatres were in London, and provincial performances were in barns or inns or from carts. If one of the family was successful, the history of the rest may have been collected (as with the Kembles and Robertsons), but for the run-of-the-mill performer, information is hard to find. One snag is that some were from respectable families, even gentry, so used false names.

Poor persons making a journey sometimes walked great distances for work or to get home to their parish. Some were taken up as criminals (if they picked a handful of wayside fruit, say) but, on the whole, if they looked respectable and were not sick or pregnant, they could shelter in a barn overnight and even get a few pence to speed them on their way. Some had an official pass which said where they were going and why, so were designated 'passengers' or 'waygoers'. If they did fall ill, they might be allowed to stay, but if they died or gave birth, the parish register would note the settlement place, to avoid future claims for settlement (and recover funeral charges, if possible). Some clergy were better than others at discovering and recording details – some just note 'a stranger' or 'a wayfaring child'.

'Travellers' in parish registers often means gipsies or other semi-permanent itinerants. Proper gipsies subsisted by fortune telling, circus tricks and – mainly – by selling horses, which they sometimes bought, sometimes stole. They covered a wide area of country to avoid retribution.

Others classed as gipsies were really travelling tradesmen, who acted as tinkers or general metal workers. They went from village to village in carts, at fairly regular intervals, mending pots, pans, and small mechanisms, including clocks. They travelled within a limited area, each family apparently having a 'territory' which was their own to work. Once established, they can readily be traced by a blanket search of all parishes in it, since they mostly were regular baptisers. Their names were often exotic, through mixing with travelling troupes of actors and hearing plays rehearsed.

Very similar were pedlars, hucksters and higglers, who took packs of small goods out to villages, or went round buying small manufactures for resale. They had set areas to work and needed licences to trade, so were known as 'badgers', from the licence badge worn. On a grander scale were chapmen, who worked the towns with sample packs of goods, and supplied customers from warehouses in one town. Few of these took families with them, but often found wives in distant places, so might re-visit.

All wanderers were treated with suspicion, but those who worked the same villages regularly were accepted as providing a useful service. Their 'poverty' was doubtful, for they would not advertise that they carried much money in their carts.

Soldiers were similarly mobile and some took their families with them. If regiment or officer is named in the parish register, you can find other towns where the family is likely to have gone, and even trace the original marriage to a girl from a far distant county. Army records may help trace the origins of soldiers who settle down where their brides came from, after leaving the army.

Official reports

Whenever poverty became a national issue, there were official persons and bodies who reported on it. Most of these reports of official commissions were published as Parliamentary papers and many contain a wealth of detail about the individuals called upon to give evidence. Every problem which became the subject for legislation – parish apprentices, poor relief allowances, children in the mines, factory conditions – had a Royal Commission report, and all are worth reading for background information, and the chance of finding actual ancestral gold. Hansard, the reports of Parliamentary proceedings, also contains speeches with personal details about constituents' problems, among a great deal of waffle about foreign policy and religious dogma. Organised migration schemes from rural to industrial areas produced official lists.

During most of the 19th century, private gentlemen and journalists were collecting evidence about the problems of the poor and much of it was published. There is a useful list of books and articles in *The Town Labourer* and *The Village Labourer* by J.L. and Barbara Hammond. Among contemporary sources are William Cobbett's *Political Register* and *Rural Rides* (early 19th century); Henry Mayhew's *London Labour and the London Poor* (1851); Friedrich Engels' *Condition of the Working Classes in England* (1844, Manchester and Sheffield); and the Reports of the Society for Bettering the Conditions of the Poor (1795–1808). A good rummage in libraries will often produce something relevant to your ancestral area or trade.

When is a pauper not a pauper?

The fact that a man signed his name with a cross doesn't prove he was a pauper. Many farmers could not write and even gentlemen were not fluent sometimes. Unless there was a village schoolmaster, fathers might not bother to educate their sons, still less their daughters. After 1870, all children should have gone to school, but some slipped the net.

For a few years from 1783, register entries of baptisms and burials may have 'pd 3d' or 'P' against them. 'P' meant pauper. The clergy had been ordered to collect a tax on entries and forward it to the government, unless the person was a pauper. They resented the work, so to frustrate the tax man, overnight, everyone not paying land tax would be offered the 'P' designation – and most took it happily.

A somewhat similar situation occurred over a century earlier, in the lists of payers of Hearth Tax. All householders were assessed, but paupers were excused paying. Some managed to avoid paying by getting themselves categorised as paupers when other sources suggest they were reasonably well-off – but friends with the assessors. In the 1660s some county lists (arranged by parish) specifically list those excused payment, and in the early 1670s there were printed forms for this purpose. The Gibson Guide to *The Hearth Tax, Other Later Stuart Tax Lists and the Association Oath Rolls* lists the surviving documents, their location (mostly in the Public Record Office, London) and transcripts or indexes.

The poor are always with us?

A family which was poor in the 19th century may have been ruined by the enclosures which did for the small farmers. It is always worth looking for wills further back, when they were affluent. Don't be put off by finding 'ag labs' wall to wall in the census. Some labourers then went to the factories or worked on the railways and struck it rich late last century – so don't imagine that comfortable incomes for the last two or three generations mean the family were never poor. Chance, good or bad health, hard work or laziness could alter the social status at any time. There are no tight compartments for classes in Britain. Most people's ancestry is a splendid mixture of rich and poor, upper class and labourers.

Tracing elusive origins

If there are no settlement papers for the parish, or if your ancestor arrived and then married a local girl, how can you find where he came from? First check the arrival parish carefully, to extract every other reference to the surname. If there are marriages of two or three others of your name, at about the same time as that of your ancestor; or if there are burials of unidentified members of the family, this may help a lot. Three siblings are easier to look for than one man. The burials may be of their parents, who moved in with an almost adult family.

In this case, assume that we found a possible marriage in 1759, which led us to the bride's family, but not to the antecedents of John Bloggs. However, we have that uncommon, unexplained name Dorcas as a clue. Also, when you comb the burial registers, an entry for 'Charles Bloggs, a young man', in 1768. 'Young' could be 19 to 30, give or take a year or so. A 'youth' is 13 to 19 (and in some areas and times can be a girl). A 'child' is up to about 12 or 13, and an infant either under two, or up to five in some places.

The old method of locating was a blanket search of the next parish on either side, then the next, and so on, outwards. Now, this may be shortened by searching the IGI. If, for instance, you found the baptism of any John Bloggs in the period 1725–40, you would consider it a possible, especially if it was within reasonable distance of Peasley. If there was a John baptised in 1736, with a brother Charles baptised in 1746, it would be quite probable, and if their mother was named Dorcas, then the balance of probability increases to 90% +. Of course, you would have to check the original registers to make sure that the selected pair did not die young, or continue in the parish of birth, or emerge elsewhere as adults. But given a good working hypothesis, it is worth studying that particular parish very closely for confirmation – though don't refuse to accept anything which upsets your theory. After all, there may be another John and Charles, son of × and Dorcas a few extra miles away.

If you found no suitable baptism of John, but a baptism of Charles to (say) William and Dorcas, or the marriage of William and Dorcas, not followed by baptisms in that parish, then study those parishes in detail. Does the parish with the Charles also happen to contain the baptism of Dorcas, daughter of John and Sarah, in 1759? Does William Bloggs leave a will naming a son John? Does the original marriage entry show that William came from a parish which is not covered by the IGI? Look at the banns as well as the marriage itself. If he was a 'sojourner in this parish', are there settlement papers for the parish of marriage, showing that he was removed back home the same year?

Ever-increasing circles

If you find nothing positive in using the IGI, even on CD-ROM, or the BVR, then it's back to the old blanket search method. Study the map of the area. If you know your man was a farm worker, then he would have been hired at an annual fair in the nearest market town (A). Work out which this is in relation to the parish he arrives at (B), and then cast a circle of about six miles round that. On the whole, farmers employed men whose families they knew for preference, so try the parishes between B and A first. The commoner the surname you are working on, the more important it is to search every local parish, and try to eliminate all the possibles but one.

If your man was in a trade, then the movement could be greater. Good craftsmen could sometimes take the risk of walking along the road and offering their services in different places till they found a job. This was usually only done by single men, who could sleep rough and stand harsh treatment from resentful locals. Certainty of finding a job was unlikely in rural areas, so this is mostly a town to town movement, along main roads.

Building trade workers are a special case. Rich men had a passion for tearing down nasty old fashioned Elizabethan manors and putting up smart Georgian piles. They often employed a crew of imported masons, carpenters, plumbers, painters and tilers, for the couple of years necessary. A man had the chance to form local attachments and stay put afterwards. The place of origin might not be local, since if the architect was a 'foreigner' he might choose to employ men who had worked with him before, in other areas.

If your ancestor was a builder of any kind, and his name is not local to the county, check if the mansion was rebuilt at the same period when he appeared. The county or local histories will show this. The *Gentleman's Magazine* may well comment. If the architect was not just a local builder, but a 'name' employed for his known abilities, check if there is a biography and find out what he was building before, even in another county. Is your ancestor's surname common in that county? Then try the IGI for that area and see if a likely family occurs. And don't forget wills – someone paid for a craftsman's apprenticeship, after all.

Listings

There are a number of records which list people in a particular place at a particular year, which may be helpful. Most of them involve persons who own property. There are, however, some more general ones, covering all males, or males of a certain age. These are the Militia Ballot lists, normally of men from 18 to 45 or 50, from which were selected two or more men to serve on behalf of a local parish in the county force. Most lists seem to have been destroyed when they became obsolete, and only the names of men selected were preserved, but a few were retained in total. For instance, there is a complete list of men, including any infirmities, for Hertfordshire in 1764 (and good coverage for other years to 1787); Northampton in 1777 (includes numbers of children). Other years have full lists for a part of a county only.

Similar listings of men 16 to 60 (1798) or 17 to 55 (1803) were made against threatened invasion. The former survives complete for Buckinghamshire only and is published as the *Posse Comitatus*. It includes details of infirmities, and of horse and cart owners and millers as well. There are extensive *Levee en Masse* lists for 1803 but none complete for a county. Dates and coverage of all such lists are in the Gibson Guide *Militia Lists and Musters 1756–1876*.

The Marriage Tax (1695–1706) on entries in parish registers, on bachelors and widowers, would be very useful, if more returns survived. Those few that do are listed in *Hearth Tax etc returns* (Gibson).

In 1641, a 'voluntary' collection was made for 'Distressed Protestants in Ireland'. Most people, including females and some children, contributed and those who did not are, in some places, listed to be leaned on later. Not all returns survive, (at the PRO Chancery Lane), but a list is published by the West Surrey FHS of those that do, with reference numbers.

In some counties, modern indexes of particular trades or groups of people have been made, or combined indexes of names in documents at the CRO. These are detailed in *Unpublished Personal Name Indexes* and *Marriage, Census and Other Indexes* (both Gibson).

Failing all other clues, if your ancestral surname is not local to the county, but is distinctive, look at Guppy's *Homes of Family Names* (found in most good references libraries). This was based on a sample of farmer's names, so it misses out on the determinedly submerged poor or the townee rich, but most families have a farmer somewhere.

Alternatively, a blanket search of the IGI and BVR for England, (and Scotland, Wales or Ireland if necessary) will show which counties have large deposits of the surname. This can be quite dramatically helpful, especially if an uncommon Christian name runs in the known family, for no ascertainable reason.

At some stage, you will discover illegitimacy in the family. It is not a stopper on research, by any means, though people in some periods are more cunning in concealing the truth.

ILLEGITIMACY

Every child has a father and mother. If the couple are not married at the time of the birth, then the child is illegitimate. There is nothing new, unusual or shocking about illegitimacy – there is a lot of it about, there always has been and probably always will be. Sooner or later, most family historians come across it among their own ancestors, unless they were very under-sexed or more cunning than average at concealment. In most cases, it is no bar to further search, since the father's name can be discovered and the hunt proceed as normal.

Some bastards are more equal than others

There always used to be a distinction in the public attitude to different sorts of bastards, according to their provenance. In descending order of acceptance:-

1. The child of a couple who intend to marry when possible (or where the man died before the wedding or deserted at the last moment).
2. The child of a stable relationship where the couple cannot (or will not) marry for a valid reason (mad wife, deserting husband, religious scruples).
3. The children of a rich man's mistress.
4. The product of causal seduction of a young girl.
5. The children of a poor man's steady mistress.
6. The children of a prostitute or promiscuous amateur.
7. The child of a married woman by another man.
8. The child of incest.

Although there was almost always a financial disadvantage (except for class 3) there was rarely much social stigma which mattered, except in the upper and middle classes. The Parson was paid to moralise and sometimes did. The Squire's spinster sister might sneer at a temptation which had never come her way, but for most ordinary folk, 'there but for the Grace of God go I'.

Attitudes hardened further up the social scale as did the handicaps, but the main blame lay in not covering up in some acceptable way. In Victorian times, this passion for concealment spread down the social scale, and it is then that illegitimacy became shameful, not to be spoken about in polite society. Even the most Victorian of maiden aunts, however, relaxes if it is suggested that the father of the child was rich, a gentleman or preferably Royal, whatever the character of the man or the association.

There has always been a double standard of morality – women are expected to behave better than men, even by the men who spend their time undermining this. Therefore, any blame going has always attached to the mother rather than the father, and it was necessary to prove to local satisfaction that she was seduced, not a tart or even a willing party. This was obviously easier in the home village, where the facts were known, than in a town. The girl who ran away from home to follow a soldier might start in class 1 to 4, but inevitably ended in class 6. The village bad girl, however, was regarded as worse than the town tart, since she was a direct threat to stable families. Even if she confined her attention to only one married man, the wives' trade union united against her and their children bullied hers. She couldn't win even if she stuck to bachelors, since they were some mothers' sons and might be forced to marry her some day.

The product of an incestuous relationship within a close family unit was treated as a leper and generally died mysteriously as an infant. There were marginal cases of incest, where the parties came within the 'prohibited degrees' listed in the prayer book, and could not marry because they were related. If a man married again in old age, his grandchildren of the first marriage and children of the last were much of an age, and illegal relationships sometimes grew up between half-uncle and niece, thrown together.

And as man and wife were one flesh, their kin occupied the same technical relationship to each other, without blood ties. If a wife died, her sister might come to help out with the children, but the widower could never marry her legally, though sometimes couples went through a ceremony where they were not known. Marriage with Deceased Wife's Sister, after being an issue throughout the 19th century, became legal, and retrospectively so, in 1908, and the children were legitimated. This accounts for many a family feud which no one will explain, for the first family regarded the second as incestuous. In certain cases, a mother would conceal the fact that her daughter's child was incestuous, to avoid the scandal, though inevitably it soured family relationships and the child, if it lived, might be 'picked on' and frightened into imbecility.

The child of a married woman is assumed to be that of her husband if they are living together, even technically. Only if he could prove long absence, for eleven months or so, or medical incapability, could a husband have this legal presumption altered. Even the king who went down in history as Enrique el Impotente jibbed at this. Unless it was such a public scandal that the parson recorded the true name of the father in the parish register, it is very difficult to discover true parentage. Very many husbands may have a vague suspicion, which the appearance of the child might tend to confirm, but few would publicise their thoughts. Family tradition may hint, but truth may be almost impossible to prove.

Pre-Victorian background

In the upper classes, the unmarried daughters and sisters represented valuable counters in the game of financial, political or territorial advancement, so they were guarded closely until such time as they could be auctioned off to the highest bidder. It was vital to have a clearly legitimate heir to a title or landed estates, so the girl must be kept a virgin till marriage, with the aid of chaperones to be with her at all times. If a girl of this class somehow evaded Papa's surveillance and became pregnant, she would be thrown out, hastily married off 'beneath her' if the man was halfway suitable, or, in the 18th century, perhaps packed off to France with a mystery illness which lasted exactly nine months. The infant would be fostered out to a lower class couple, with expenses paid and possibly some provision when the child was 14. The arrangements were normally conducted through a friend or lawyer, and only rarely was it possible for a child to find out the truth, unless the mother blew her own cover, through idle curiosity or pangs of conscience. The exceptional bright or pretty child was sometimes taken into the natural family as 'ward' or 'nephew'.

Below this level, there might be some manipulation by a farmer to limit the range of his daughter's acquaintance – as there is today – to other farmers' sons, but once she had selected a suitable young man, restrictions were lifted. The betrothed couple enjoyed most of the privileges of the married couple, and if the girl became pregnant, they might accelerate the wedding, or might not, if they were busy with the harvest. As long as the bride made it up the church steps before she went into labour, all was well. If she became involved with an unsuitable young man, Father might refuse his consent or make the best of it and allow the marriage, or support the girl and her child till someone better came along. One illegitimate child was neither here nor there, especially for a girl with a dowry.

Among ordinary labourers, the illegitimacy rate was inevitably higher, since even a couple who wished to marry there and then might not be able to. The relationship remained, and they mostly married later, before the second, or maybe the third, child was due. A young male labourer often lived in at the farmhouse, and neither there nor in the overcrowded family cottage was there room for a wife and child. It was simple commonsense for a local girl to stay unmarried, rather than wed an incomer with no settlement in the village and risk being thrown out with him and the baby, if he lost his job or health.

Casual sex occurred commonly between young people at 'maying' time, when young people spent the night in the woods and came home covered in may blossom and blushes. Also at harvest and Christmas, when the farmers gave feasts and alcohol loosened inhibitions; and during haying, when the climate was agreeable and the piles of hay to hand and a lot of temporary labourers were around. If a local couple were involved they might marry and make the best of it – even a reasonable success. But no one expected a local girl to wed some roving Welsh or Irish labourer just to 'give the baby a name', when it would have her perfectly good local name.

Similarly, no one seriously expected the couple to marry if their social class was very unequal. If the Squire's son, or a rich farmer's, got a girl in the family way, he had to pay up, not marry the girl. Often, the pay-off gave a poor girl a dowry which facilitated her marriage to the poor man she preferred anyway – which is why the blame was sometimes put on the man who could afford it, rather than the real father. On the whole, stepfathers seem to have accepted a genuine child of a rich man, cheerfully enough, as a present financial asset and a possible future lever against landlord or employer.

Official attitudes

The clergy had a professional duty to reprimand 'incontinency' among their flock, but most of them were close enough in background to the farming community they served to accept what was natural, and they reserved their criticism for the prostitute, or for rape and incest. Strictly, a couple who produced a bastard child had to do penance in a white sheet in the church porch (in extreme cases in the market place). The churchwardens had a duty to 'present' cases of immorality before the bishop's apparitor, when that official made his annual rounds. The presentments are recorded in the bishop's registers and sometimes on the foot of the parchment containing the bishop's transcript of the parish registers. The custom bore most heavily on dissenters and others unpopular with the establishment.

There were more compelling reasons for taking an interest in the parentage of a bastard than moral ones. Each parish had to care for its own poor, which normally included the unmarried mother and her child, so it required to know all about the case, with details of the father's name and origins, with the intention of claiming back some of the expenditure from him. The parish records are the first place to look for the parentage of bastards.

Parish registers

There are numerous ways of expressing illegitimacy:

Latin: ignotus = unknown (father).
    spurius = spurious, occasionally with the father's name alone given.
    filius populi = son of the people; appears to cover cases where the father is local, but might be one of two.
    filius nullius = son of none; seems to cover cases where the father was a stranger or the girl can't or won't say.
English: base, bastard, spurious, supposed, imputed, misbegotten, chance begotten.

'Baptised John son of Mary Brown and the reputed son of John Smith'
means he admits it, or it has been proved.
'Baptised John ..., the imputed son of John Smith' means she says so, but
he won't admit it, or the case is not settled yet.

A common way of showing paternity is to give the male child his father's
full name and the girl his surname. The idea is that if the couple marry later,
the mother's surname can be dropped.

John Smith son of Mary Brown and John Smith is legally known as John
Smith Brown until the wedding, and maybe after, if it is much delayed. An
apparent double-barrelled name is therefore suspect, if it occurs anywhere
but in a recognised gentry family before about 1840. In London, Lancashire,
Yorkshire and among nonconformists, the use of a complementary second
surname, from the mother's family, the pastor, or a rich uncle, came in in the
early parts of the 1800s, and generally later in the Victorian period, until it
was commonplace, and is very useful to genealogists, but before this, or
outside the named areas, check for illegitimacy.

An earlier example of a genuine double surname might arise where a
gentry family inherited the name of an old aristocratic family through their
heiresses, sometimes compounded, as in Twisleton-Wykeham-Fiennes. This
is very rare. Late in the 19th century, people with very common names
sometimes invented a similar hyphenated surname for themselves
(Armstrong-Jones, or Heygate-Browne). This shows snobbery (or pride in
ancestry), not illegitimacy.

The printed forms in use for registers after 1813 left no real room for
entering an illegitimate father's name. Some of the clergy gave up, but some
managed, nonetheless.

Date	Name of child	Name of parents	Occupation
Jan 5	John Brown	Jane Smith	base
Jan 5	John Brown	Jane Smith	spinster
		and John Brown	labourer
Jan 5	John	Jane Smith	servant
		and John Brown,	base child
		labourer,	
Jan 5	John	John Brown	labourer
		& Jane Smith	

The last entry leaves it in doubt – are they married? Is the man's name John
Brown Smith, an earlier bastard perhaps? Check the marriage registers and
later baptisms for the same couple, or earlier baptisms to see if John Brown
Smith exists.

After 1837, it becomes increasingly rare for the actual registers to record
the father's name at all, in deference to growing prudery. It is always worth
looking at marriage registers, though, since many bastards were told who
their father was at that point, and quoted it to the parson. Occasionally, a

legitimate brother or sister would come along as a witness – rarely, even the father, if he lived locally. One very good reason for telling the child his name was that otherwise, the bastard might fall in love with a half-sister, legitimate or illegitimate.

Other parish records

If the register entry says merely
    'Baptised John son of Mary Brown a baseborn child'
then other sources must be tried. Documents which would have been in the parish chest come first.

Each parish was responsible for its own poor, so when it looked probable that some village girl was expecting a baby, they made enquiries. Unmarried mothers had few possibilities of supporting themselves unless they were kept by a rich man or became prostitutes, which was profitable but short-lived, and ruined any chance of marriage later. Therefore they mostly became chargeable on the parish.

A bastard was the responsibility of the parish where it was born, so the sharper parishes tended to throw out any girl who looked pregnant. Later, they agreed to retain one who was their own settled inhabitant, but sent strangers back to their own parishes of settlement, encouraged by a whip if necessary. The girl had to admit who the father was. Mostly this would be known anyway in a village, unless it was a one night stand. She could even be sent to prison if she refused to tell.

The young man was then sent for and shown the girl's Examination, which named him. He was also questioned, to see if he admitted paternity on the spot. He could:

a. Pay the girl enough privately to keep her and the child (which he could do before it came to the overseers' attention, and so keep his name out of it).
b. He could pay the overseers a minimum of £40 down, representing £2 for the lying-in and a shilling a week for 14 years, plus a sum to ensure that the only mention might be in the overseers' accounts:
    'From John Smith about the lying in of Mary Brown'.
    A persuasive man might even keep his name out of the parish registers, though most clergy did insist on showing it, if only for the sake of avoiding future incest.
c. Admit paternity and sign a Bastardy Bond, which promised to pay the lying-in expenses and maintenance at some date in the future, hoping the child would die young. If it died within three weeks of birth, the bond was rescinded.
d. Admit nothing or deny it all. The overseers might talk him round, take him before the local magistrate, bring witnesses, set the girl's brothers on him or otherwise pressure him. He might then agree to marry the girl, with perhaps a few shillings as a sweetener from the parish, but if he still refused to sign, he would be committed to the Assizes.

e. Refuse to admit it and abscond. The parish would try to track him down, and there were a number of forms to cover this process, plus details of expenditure in the accounts. If brought back, the next stage would be to pressure locally and then the Assizes.
f. Be brought to trial at the Assizes. It took a very determined man, with a great many witnesses to prove he was elsewhere at the time involved, to escape conviction. If he had been seen with the girl at around the right time, that was it. There were no blood tests.

   The first record will show the complaint:
   'Henry Barret and James Linford, Overseers of the Poor of the parish of Slowly, against John Smith. They allege that Mary Brown an inhabitant thereof is with child and that the child is likely to be born a bastard and that she doth swear the aforesaid John Smith is the father thereof.'

   After an interval, the next report is:
   'That Mary Brown of Slowly has been brought to bed of a male bastard child on the fourth of June last past and that John Smith of Surely is the father of the said child.'

   The upshot is that he is convicted, signs the Bastardy Bond and pays up, possibly after a period in prison awaiting trial.
g. Run for it and join the Army or Navy. Service in the Royal forces was a bar against prosecution. If the process had already started, the date and place of enlistment and the name of the man's officer and regiment will be entered in the Assize roll. The latter records are mostly at County Record Offices as Quarter Sessions records, and some have been printed or indexed in annual sections.

Even when a man had signed the bond or been convicted, the parish still had to get the money from him. If he was poor, but had a father who was well-to-do, then the father might be asked to countersign the bond and guarantee payment. If there were no rich relations, the man's parish would be asked to pay. This might not be where he happened to be living at the moment, but was his parish of settlement, from which he could claim support in time of trouble. Another series of forms will cover the attempt of the girl's parish to discover the man's legal parish and get money from them. There were 20 possible forms printed to cope with all the ins and outs of bastardy and another dozen for settlement questions. All of these would have been in the parish chest.

Another document which may assist is an apprenticeship indenture – possibly among other parish chest papers, if the child was a parish (poor) apprentice, but probably now at the County Record Office. Some natural fathers took an interest – especially if the child was a boy – and paid for his apprenticeship to a good trade. A counter-signature on the indenture, for no apparent reason, may be a clue to parentage, though it is not evidence enough by itself.

Nonconformists

The entries of baptisms in chapel registers rarely show the name of the father of a bastard, probably because immoral behaviour was regarded more strictly, and the registers were far more open to inspection than church ones then, so no (male) clerk wanted to brand a male member of the flock with such a charge, for all to see. There is generally some comment in the minute books of the chapel, since the girl (and, rarely, the man too) would be called before the elders and made to confess to her terrible wickedness. These minute books may be at the chapel, or deposited in the CRO. Very few exist before 1800, and those that do have sometimes been printed, as rarities.

Before 1837, there were some hardy chapel folk who refused to go to church even for weddings. Before 1754, an ordained priest could marry them. Some of the chapel pastors had been ordained in the past, and seen the error of their ways, so they could and did marry their flock. After 1754, only marriage by a beneficed clergyman in a licensed church (normally the parish church) was legal, except for Quakers and Jews, whose records were much better than the average church's. Some other nonconformists continued to marry before their own pastors, and fewer of these were ex-Church of England clergy or even from the minor orders of clergy. These marriages were illegal and the children illegitimate, except in the eye of God. Unfortunately, it wasn't the Anglican God from whom all blessings flowed, including personal property, so when it came to inheritance of the father's estate, neither 'wife' nor children were entitled to take it. This meant either that the father had to make an exceedingly watertight will, leaving his estate to his 'wife' as 'Mary Jones now known as Mary Robinson by repute' and branding his children as bastards, or that they had to find a church which would marry them without forcing them to be baptised first. The latter course was safer where real estate was concerned, since a brother who did not share the man's religious principles might challenge the children's inheritance of it. A great deal of property was entailed to 'my son X and his heirs lawful for ever', and the offspring of these pastor-married unions were not lawful within the meaning of the act.

Most counties had several 'places of resort' where the clergyman of a small parish was happy to turn an honest penny by marrying anyone to anyone, if his palm was crossed with silver. Most got in job lots of marriage licences, which the intending couple could buy and marry on the spot. This got over the need to have banns called in the local parish church and thus give time for pressure towards baptism to mount.

Obviously, if a family had no property (or real estate) at all, they might risk a chapel 'marriage', but the poorer they were, the more likely they were to need parish relief, and this was heavily geared to conventional (and church-going) families. Children born as 'bastards' could be sent back to the parish of their birth for support, which could split a family up. On the whole, most chapels agreed to let their members marry according to the law, after 1754.

Alias names in parish registers

Often you will find a family surname expressed as 'Smith alias (or als) Jones'. Obviously, the most common reason for this is illegitimacy, normally where the father has publicly acknowledged the child as his. It also occurs in nonconformist families where there has been only a chapel wedding. The person(s) involved and the legitimate descendants may use one name at one time and the other, or the complete alias, at others. He can settle on one after a few years, or on moving to a new parish where the double version is unknown.

There are other reasons for an alias name, for a legitimate child. A young child brought up by a stepfather, grandparents or an uncle will tend to be known by the name of the head of the household, and may have some trouble reverting to his own. An apprentice or long-term employee might be known by the name of his master or of the place where he worked. The second surname might be taken as an adult under the terms of a will, in particular by the son in law or grandson of a man with no male heir of his own. It could be a simple spelling variant (Messenger alias Massingberd) or represent indecision between a locative and an occupational surname (Hathaway alias Gardener). People who come in with a foreign surname are very likely to have it altered to fit local tongues (Lefebure alias Feaver, Teinturier alias Dyer). Some of these occur very early. Families of Welsh descent on the borders may dither between keeping the father's surname and altering it to a patronymic.

Victorian attitudes

Under the new Poor Law of 1834, the poor were no longer the sole responsibility of their parish of settlement, but collectively of their 'Union' of a group of parishes. 'Out-relief' – paying allowances to paupers in their own homes, and the rent if necessary – was largely ended and the poor were shovelled into the Union workhouse, which might be miles from home. Workhouse masters were often cruel and grasping. Strangers and pregnant girls, like the aged, sick and widows, were bullied and made to feel ashamed of poverty. Unless their families could or would help, the workhouse it had to be – and a baby who survived that sort of beginning was tough. Not all workhouse records are complete or survive at all, but if so, they are likely to be at the County Record Office or large town library.

The father of the child might be taken to court, at the Petty Sessions, and the case reported in lurid detail in the local papers. As time wore on, surface morality made this publicity something which those who could do so would pay anything to avoid. The tougher men would horsewhip editors who offended too, which meant that by the end of the century, only cases involving poor persons were reported and only if they had 'interesting' details. In the 20th century, such 'domestic' cases tended not to be reported normally, and now the trend is to mention cases concerning the rich and famous only.

The most important commandment in Victorian times was 'Thou shalt not be Found Out'. The manoeuvres which the upper classes had always used to conceal an indiscretion now spread to the middle and lower middle classes. Those who could afford it went abroad or far from home. Mother might pad herself up to simulate pregnancy and take over her daughter's child, which was plausible enough for the eldest but sometimes carried to ridiculous lengths to cover for a younger daughter. The locals might be suspicious, but the child might believe Granny was Mother until he was adult. Frequently, the truth might not be told till the child married (or at all), or on the mother's deathbed. But sometimes the revelation was forced because a romantic attachment grew between those who had a parent in common.

Victorians had a number of euphemisms for illegitimacy to avoid saying the dreadful word bastard.

In former times you will find a child described in a will as 'natural' if he is the own child of a testator, not a stepchild. The legal expression, 'natural and lawful', was just the usual repetition, but Victorians seemed to think it was an alternative (a 'natural' also meant an idiot in their terms).

Other terms for the child are: left-hand; chance child; come-by-chance; misbegotten; love-child; mistake; bye-blow; slip; incubus; on the wrong side of the blanket; sinister.

The mother was: in trouble; up the stick or the spout; in a certain condition; fallen; slipped; tripped; unfortunate; lost; broken-kneed/winged/ or legged; ruined; had strayed or sinned.

In this sort of climate, the revelation that a girl was going to have a baby 'without a father' produced shock waves. Small wonder that she would often delay telling the family until it was too late to consider abortion by taking a herbal draught, which had been used by some in earlier days, though the dangers and unreliability of the method deterred most girls.

The only palliative was rapid marriage, to the father or anyone who offered, however unsuitable, and a carefully staged 'premature' birth. Where the family had any local pretensions, even small ones, the girl would other-wise be sent away, thrown out entirely or encouraged to find a home elsewhere, possibly with a lowly relative, masquerading as a widow.

In London, it was possible to find anonymity, and perhaps a mechanical abortion. Given a little money, a place in one of the lodging houses or charity Homes for Fallen Women could be found. The private houses were often spotting grounds for likely prostitutes, so the innocent girl who had once been seduced might have no chance to get back on the straight and narrow. The old song *She was Poor but she was Honest* is a very fair summing up of the likely career of a village girl who 'lost her honest name' and went to London.

Official records

A standard birth certificate after 1837 for a bastard normally shows the mother's name and occupation, with a blank where the father's name should be. If the father actually went along with the mother and signed the notification, then his name would be entered too – but not if she gave it alone. A married woman's name is written as 'Mary Smith formerly Jones', but the mother on this sort of certificate is given her maiden name alone, 'Mary Jones'. The legal surname would be that of the mother, but if the couple later married, the father's name might be consistently used as an adult. If you find an ancestor with no birth registration, try the mother's maiden name (from the birth certificate of a younger sibling) and see if the ancestor was registered as that.

A determined couple could pretend to be married when they were not, and register the children as legitimate. In the country, someone would probably let the official know, sooner or later, but in a town, especially in London, no-one knew or cared, unless the children tried to claim an inheritance, and had to show the non-existent marriage certificate.

Occasionally, one or both of the couple changed names to avoid detection by the legal spouse or the police. This is difficult, though sometimes the disguise is a transparent one, like reversing their surnames, or using his mother's surname. Even when a new name was chosen, it might have some link with the old home and often the initials were retained.

Census records should be consulted for persons alive by early 1891 and the 1881 census is fully indexed by personal name. Where the mother married after the birth of her child, you will want to know if the new husband is the natural father or not. The census entry may refer to the child as 'son', or 'son-in-law' (stepson) or 'wife's son', which settles the matter. In 1841, no relationships are stated, but the stepchild will retain the old name in this document usually, and may be put out of sequence at the end of the family. A kindly man may treat him in every way as a son, which confuses the issue rather.

If you can locate the family in 1901 (for which the census is not public till 2002), it is possible to buy limited information, but only of the age and birthplace of a named person at a stated address, not relationships. If he is out, you lose your money – and as it costs £34, this is not worth doing often.

If you can locate the child as an infant in an earlier census, it is worth noting down men with the same Christian name (and certainly any with his middle surname, if this is given). For a girl, there is less Christian name evidence, though sometimes the father's mother will have taken an interest – or the baby's mother will have had the nerve to use her name for this 'left hand' grandchild.

After 1891, there are a few other official records which help. If you know where the girl was nine months before the baby's birth, find out who was in the house, from electoral rolls or rating records, or street directories. Try to trace the actual house where the baby was born too, and try to assess its size – mother may have been a servant there or a lodger, and the owner is not necessarily the culprit, but can be checked on.

Electoral rolls should be at the town or county record office. They will include owners of property and major tenants only until 1914, when all adult males are listed, regardless of status. Females are not listed until 1918 and only those over 30 until 1928. From then onwards, the rolls are good evidence of cohabitation in the simple sense.

Legitimation

If the parents of a bastard child married subsequently, he was by custom regarded as a legitimate child and assumed his father's name, although sometimes special provision had to be made for him to inherit property which was devised to 'heirs lawful of the body' of so and so. He could not inherit a title, however. Sometimes the eldest sons of peers who had married too late contested this point – especially if there had been a fake marriage to seduce the mother initially – and the case was fully reported by the House of Lords. The 'secret marriage' at an earlier date would be claimed but not proven and the younger brothers would inherit. Occasionally there had been a genuine marriage abroad, but if it wasn't performed by an Anglican clergyman and reported back, it didn't count. Most couples who married abroad did marry again in England, if they had any property to leave.

Adoptions

The taking over of responsibility for another man's child by a stepfather, grandfather, uncle, employer or other person was formerly done without formality. Stepchildren were mostly assimilated into the family and even took the stepfather's name, as well as, or instead of, their own. Grandparents or married sisters might bring up the children of an unmarried girl as their own. Masters, especially childless ones, adopted promising apprentices and academics bright children from the lower classes. A few men even adopted female children to train them up as suitable future wives. Except, perhaps, for the last class, the adoption probably worked out to the advantage of the child. There was no legislation to control adoption until 1926.

Family traditions

Very often, it was not much of a secret who the father of a bastard was. The child would be told as an adult, at marriage, at the mother's deathbed. Or, if a possible romantic association with a half-brother or sister seemed likely. Incest overcame prudery. However, sometimes family traditions are downright lies, or wishful thinking.

Even the most prudish of Victorian aunts would accept the awful shame of illegitimacy as long as the father was a gentleman – the local squire, or, preferably, a member of the Royal family. This encouraged a scared girl to name the wrong man and for families to fake such a descent many years later. The number of children that George III is supposed to have had by Hannah Lightfoot would be difficult to fit into that Quaker girl's brief life, apart from her respectable though non-Quaker marriage to Isaac Axford. A lot of bastards claimed Royal descent after reading the pamphlets of 'Princess Olive of Cumberland' (Mrs Serres), a brilliant forger and romantic genealogist. If the family tradition comes only from an aunt with a weakness for romantic novels, forget it.

Even when the tradition is old, inspect it carefully. Is the suggested father old enough? Did he live in the same place, or come into contact with the girl at the right time? If Granny was a maid at the Manor, she might well have fallen a victim to the wicked Squire or his son – but equally, the butler, or the bootboy or the gamekeeper might have done it. Try to compare a photograph of the child with portraits of the rest of the nominal family and with the Squire's family. If he looks quite unlike the one and very like the other, then this is corroboration but not proof. He might hark back to an earlier ancestor (who might, of course, really be a bastard of an earlier Squire).

If a rich man dun it, there was generally a pay-off. If the mother was set up in a shop or bought a husband, if the child received a mystery gift to apprentice him, if there was sudden improvement in the financial status of a girl from a poor family, someone with money is likely to have been involved – rarely just out of charitable impulse. If you have a name, check the man's will – a surprising number of pre-Victorian men conscientiously looked after their bastards. Even some later wills are frank about 'my baseborn son' or leave sums to 'the boy known as William Harris' or to 'William son of Mary wife of John Green'. This could be sheer benevolence, but this usually expresses itself in general charitable bequests, not legacies to one child of one woman. Some men left money on trust, through a solicitor, or felt they had done enough with the initial payment.

Collections of gentry family diaries, either published or deposited in the record office, are worth combing for indiscreet references at the time. Spinster relatives sometimes took an interest in pretty bastards of the men of the family, from religious duty. Old records deposited by solicitors may reveal mystery payments which cover attempts at blackmail or conscience money.

If the presumed father was 'in society', it is practically certain that any scandal about him will figure in the published diaries or correspondence of known gossips – like Pepys, Evelyn, Horace Walpole or Creevey (himself the bastard of Lord Sefton). A chatty book of reminiscences may give the game away about friends. Negative evidence, that a putative father was exploring the Zambesi for the whole year concerned, is as useful in settling matters.

'If I had my rights . . .'

Even if you can prove to your own satisfaction that Grandpa was the illegitimate son of a Duke, you cannot go off and claim the title. Bastardy is an absolute bar to that. The Victorians called it the 'bar sinister', after the practice of granting the coat of arms with, sometimes, a diagonal bend (not a bar), to a promising bastard of a peer. You cannot use a coat of arms like this unless the College of Arms grants it, at vast expense.

If a rich man left his estate to 'all my children', in the past a bastard son could not claim a share. Legally, he did not exist. Children are by definition legitimate children. A man wishing to leave money or property to a bastard had better use one of the phrases like 'my baseborn son'; 'the child known as William Brown'; 'my children which I had by Elizabeth Harris spinster, known as Tom, Dick and Harry Harris or Jones'.

If a bastard was left property under a will, but for some reason did not claim it, his legitimate descendents might be able to under certain circumstances, provided time had not run out under the Statute of Limitations. If he died before the testator, the legacy would have lapsed anyway. The bastard could inherit from his mother, if there were no legitimate children, but not through her from a grandparent, unless he were specifically named.

A mistress and children, however lavishly supported in the man's lifetime, had no claim at all after his death, unless he had already made provision by a settlement or trust. If it was a secret trust, whereby a friend was given money 'for the purpose of which he knows', the friend could default without redress, unless a signed contract promised payment.

Legitimated children can claim under a will or clause which comes into operation after they are legitimated, or anyway from 1969. Adopted children belong to the adoptive family, not the natural one, so cannot claim from the natural father's estate even if they are legitimate children.

Basically, forget about making money from finding your real parents/ grandparents. Let knowledge be its own reward.

Scotland

The situation in Scotland is similar to that for nonconformists. They were far stricter about illicit sex officially, and although arrangements for the poor were slightly different, moral pressure ensured that the parish wanted full details about who did what with whom among the heather. The 'examinations' are recorded in the Kirk Sessions Books, a sort of parish minute book deposited with the registers at New Register House, Edinburgh. The guilty parties had to sit on the stool of repentence before the assembled congregation for a number of Sundays, according to the gravity of the offence.

However, in the 19th century, the system of housing male farm servants and even females in bothies or chambers separate from the farmhouse gave licence rein, and illegitimacy soared. Female farm labourers managed because they could have their children with them – domestics lost their place with their honour.

The situation was complicated by the custom of 'handfast marriage'. If a couple stated before two witnesses that they intended to marry, and took hands on it, they were married with the force of law, for all purposes except inheritance of titles and some property. These irregular marriages may never have been recorded, yet be perfectly legal. Later there was provision for registration with the sheriff clerk. The marriage was not legal in England, so couples crossing the border had better marry formally. The custom is still in force, and any couple living together are regarded as married 'by habit and

A Bastardy Bond

Edited transcript of the facsimile handwritten original opposite, reproduced by kind permission of the P.C.C. of Wendover from a document now deposited in the County Record Office. Printed forms were later available for the purpose.

Know All Men by these presents that We William Playstow Junr. Son of William Playstow senr. of Lee Als. Lea in the County of Bucks. Gentleman And Richard Dell of Wendover in the sd. County of Bucks. Collermaker Are held and Firmly bound Unto Thomas Benning of Wendover Yeoman and Joseph Parnam of Wendover Yeoman Churchwardens of the parish of Wendover and Robert Kipping of Wendover Gentleman William Picton of Wendover Carpenter and William Collet of Wendover Gentleman Overseers of the poor of the parish of Wendover in the sum of Fourty pounds of Lawfull Money of Great Britaine To be paid to the said Thomas Benning Joseph Parnam Robert Kipping William Pickton and William Collet their Successors Attorneys Executors Administrators or Assigns To Which payment well and truely to be made We bind us and both of us by himself for the whole and in the whole Our and both of Our Heirs Executors and Administrators Firmly by these presents Sealed with our Seals dated the Twentysixth day of April in the sixth Year of the Reigne of our Sovraigne Lord George the Second by the Grace of God of Great Britaine France and Ireland King Defender of the Faith &c In the Year of our Lord God 1733.

The Condition of this Obligation is Such That Whereas Mary Wesson of the parish of Wendover Single Woman (daughter of Joseph Wesson of Wendover Butcher) hath of Late been delivered of a female Bastard Child within the parish of Wendover and hath made Oath before Two of his Majestys Justices of the peace for this County that the within Bounden William Playstow Junr. is the Father of the said Bastard Child, If therefore the said William Playstow and the above bound Richard Dell or either of them do and shall from time to time and at all times fully and clearly acquitt and discharge Save harmless and Indemnifie as well the above named Church Wardens and overseers of the poor their successors for the time being as also the Inhabitants and parishioners of the parish of Wendover from all Manner of Expences Costs and Charges which shall at any time hereafter Arise happen by reason of the Birth Maintenance Education and Bringing up of the said Bastard child . . .

John Senior	Will. Plaistowe Jun.
Richd. Bigg	Richard Dell

Know all Men by these presents That We William Playstone Junr. Son of William Playstone ... of ... in the County of Bucks Gentleman And Richard Goll of Wendover in the said County of Bucks Fellmonger ... held and firmly bound unto Thomas Fleming of Wendover aforesaid in the said County of Bucks Yeoman and Joseph Parsham of the parish of Wendover aforesaid Yeoman Churchwardens of the parish of Wendover aforesaid Also Robert Kipping of Wendover aforesaid ... William Pickton of Wendover aforesaid Carpenter and William Tollet of the parish of Wendover aforesaid Gentlemen Overseers of the poor of the parish of Wendover aforesaid in the sum of Fourty pounds of Lawful Money of Great Britain to be paid to the said Thomas Fleming Joseph Parsham Robert Kipping William Pickton and William Tollet their Successors ... ... or assigns To Which payment well and truly to be made We bind us and both of us by himself for the whole and in the whole Our and Both of Our Heirs Executors and Administrators firmly by these presents Sealed with Our hands Dated the Twenty sixth day of April, in the sixth Year of the Reigne of our ... Lord George the Second by the Grace of God of Great Britaine France and Ireland King Defender of the faith &c In the Year of our Lord God 1733

The Condition of this Obligation is Such That whereas one Mary Wopson of the parish of Wendover being a Woman ... Daughter of Joseph Wopson of the parish of Wendover aforesaid ... ... hath of Late been Delivered of a female Bastard Child within the parish of Wendover within ... ... hath made Oath before Two of His Majestys Justices of the peace for the County that the within named Thomas William playstone Junr. is the father of the said Bastard Child If therefore the said William playstone and Richard Goll their ... ... both or Either of them, their ... Either of their Heirs Executors or ... do and shall from time to time and at all times ... ... indemnify and save harmless ... Indemnified as well the above Named Thomas Fleming Joseph Parsham Robert Kipping William Pickton and William Tollet Churchwardens and overseers of the poor of the parish of Wendover aforesaid and their Successors for the time being and Every of them As also all the Inhabitants and parishioners of the said parish of Wendover aforesaid Which now are or hereafter shall be for the time being and Every of them of and from all and all Manner of ... Costs and Charges whatsoever which shall or may at any time hereafter Arise happen come grow or be Imposed upon them or Either or any of them for or by reason or means of the Birth Maintenance Education and Bringing up of the said Bastard Child and of and from all Actions Suits ... Damages and Demands whatsoever touching or concerning the same Then this Obligation shall be Void and of None Effect Or Else shall Remaine ... and ... shall ... in ... ...

Sealed and Delivered in
the presence of being first duly stampt

John Louior
Rich'd Brigg

Will Playstone Jun

Richard Goll

repute'. The custom extended to England much later as a 'common law marriage' – which isn't legal but gives claim to maintenance by court order.

There were a great many problems with regard to succession to property and old peerage titles of Scottish nobility (peerages of the United Kingdom could be claimed by clearly legitimate heirs only) and only the very determined got anywhere with claims to these from a handfast marriage. But for ordinary purposes, the children are not bastards at all. Obviously, there could not be a handfast marriage while one of the parties had a lawful spouse alive.

PROFESSIONALS AND MEN OF PROPERTY

The Army and Navy

James Allan Bloggs married a Maynard, and her cousin and uncle were clergymen, continuing a much earlier connection with the Church. Her grandfather, a wealthy farmer, married the daughter of an army captain, from a younger branch of a decayed gentry family who served variously in army and navy. This leads to extra sources of information.

Almost all Army and Navy records are held at the Public Record Office, Kew. Excellent leaflets are available there about the classes of documents which may be consulted. They will now be sent to enquirers if the class is specified (Army other ranks WW1, Naval officers pre 1914) or they can be downloaded from the PRO website.

Any officer in the Army or Navy will be reasonably well documented; other ranks may also be. Records of enlistment, physical descriptions, clues to birthplaces, and evidence of career can be found if the regiment is known, since Musters, Paylists etc are available. Discharge certificates, for pensioners and others, exist from 1756 to 1883, filed in alphabetical order, and they state birthplace. Men who died in service have similar details in the Paylist for the date they died. Widows' Pension lists (from 1735) may include proof of marriage and sometimes birth. Applications for Chelsea Hospital from 1715 (and Kilmainham Hospital in Ireland) include careers. Casualty returns list birthplace and next of kin.

Chaplains' Returns from 1795 contain births, marriages and deaths abroad or in British camps of Army families 'on the strength', which implies marriage with permission and residence in Army lines. These and other regimental registers are indexed separately at the FRC and in full collections of GRO indexes, as 'Miscellaneous'. These indexes state regiments, which lead to the Muster books.

Officers appear in the *Army Lists* printed since 1754 and there are published compilations of most names back to the 17th century (the Guildhall Library has all these). At the PRO, *Services of Retired Officers* (1828) may include evidences of birth, marriage and residence. There are similar lists for serving officers from 1829–1919, including date and place of birth and they are card-indexed. Officers' marriage details are recorded from 1810.

Various PRO leaflets dealing with different aspects of the Army and *Army Records for Family Historians* (Simon Fowler, PRO) are recommended. If you do not know the regiment, but know a parish where one baptism occurred, it may be possible to work it out from details of which regiment served where at the right time.

Naval officers are also well documented, with *Navy Lists* since 1749 and numerous books of biography. Passing Certificates for Naval Lieutenants exist from 1691 and from 1789 include a birth certificate as evidence that the man was 23 – though some are fictitious. Records of Services show ages, parentage and birthplaces of officers serving from 1799–1854, as well as career details. Warrant Officers, like bosuns, engineers, chief carpenters etc, are included in some of these. Surgeons, masters, engineers and clerks have records of their own.

For ratings, the ship must be known – any ship, which will lead to others. The Ship's Muster (from 1660) could show age, birthplace, and the related Description Books the man's appearance. Log Books may give personal information too. For men killed in action, there are Bounty Lists with petitions from widows and orphans.

Naval Records for Genealogists by N. A. M. Rodger and PRO leaflets are recommended.

Royal Marines have very similar records at Kew, held in three divisions, for Plymouth, Chatham and Portsmouth, from 1750 onwards. There is a PRO leaflet about these. There is a surprising amount of inland services, quelling riots. See *Records of the Royal Marines* (Garth Thomas).

Merchant Navy records: Although there are not a great many records before 1800, ship masters are usually in a position to leave wills. All of these had to be proved in the Prerogative Court of Canterbury and you will usually find the name, the ship and 'Pts' meaning 'Parts beyond the Seas' in the indexes.

Lloyd's List from the 1840s and the official Merchant Navy Officers' List from 1868 show details of ships, masters (who were certificated from 1845) and mates with masters' tickets. Lloyd's Captain's registers (1868–1947) are at the Guildhall Library (with much other Lloyd's material), and give date and place of birth, certificate number, details of voyages and death date. The Certificates, and all other official material are at the PRO Kew, though after 1861, only samples of the information are retained. A lot of important data is kept in Newfoundland!

Although crew lists were supposed to be kept from 1747, very few survive except for Dartmouth ships and a few rather later for Liverpool and Plymouth. From 1835, Crew Lists and Agreements should exist for larger or foreign-going ships. Not all the names are necessarily genuine. There is a Register of Seamen from 1835 and Tickets were issued from 1844, giving the man's date and place of birth and type of service. These are indexed.

The *New Sailors' Magazine* (1827–61 under various name changes) includes a great deal of information about voyages and shipwrecks and contains the occasional personal interview with sailors, all with a heavily religious commentary. The British Library holds what remains of the issues.

The Tower Hamlets' Local Studies Reference Library, 277 Bancroft Rd, London E1 4DQ has a specialist collection on docks, the sea and ships which is well worth consulting.

Clergymen

If you find someone described just as a 'clerk' before about 1870, he is probably a Clerk in Holy Orders, or Church of England clergyman, not a parish clerk (*my* or *our* clerk) or office clerk (scrivener or writer). Most of the clergy from about 1600 to 1850 attended Oxford or Cambridge Universities, and details of their career and parentage may be found in the *Alumni Oxonienses* or *Alumni Cantabrigienses*, student lists of which your county reference library may hold copies. In the north, Durham or Edinburgh may apply. For clergy alive in 1800–22, consult the *Index Ecclesiasticus* (J. Foster). There were Clergy Lists from c1830 and Crockford's *Clerical Directory* was published from 1858.

All Anglican clergy on ordination as priests had to produce baptismal certificates (to show they were 23) and evidences of character, social recommendations etc, which will be in the Bishop's Registry of the diocese concerned (or the Diocesan Record Office, often identical with the CRO). Many churches have a board with past clergy and their degrees etc displayed and county histories may give career details. Many published sermons or homilies which sometimes give family details, *The Dictionary of National Biography* is top-heavy with entries of clerics of even limited distinction in their time.

Non-conformist clergy may not be university men at all. The ejected Puritan clergy of 1662 are listed in Matthews' volumes, *Walker* and *Calamy Revised*. Many 'causes' have printed histories which include details of prominent pastors and elders, especially those who suffered persecution. Until after about 1835 there were few theological training colleges, and information about individual pastors should be sought from the denominational archives. Dr Williams' Library has excellent records of Independent (Congregational) clergy in particular, and good obituaries were always published e.g. in the *Arminian Magazine* (Methodist) or *Baptist Year Book*. There may be purely local memorials of small chapel causes. The Historical Society and/or Archives of the denomination should know exactly what is available, some of which will be in their own hands.

Local newspapers are excellent sources. What the clergy did and said was usually well reported at the time in the local papers. They also usually carry detailed obituaries of Anglican clergy and of many nonconformists too. These will usually state origins – important, since clergy were highly mobile people.

Doctors

Physicians, surgeons and midwives had to be licensed by the bishop, so names should appear in episcopal registers. A *Medical Directory or Register* was published from 1845.

Physicians were generally better educated. By the late 1700s, many were graduates of a University, though often of Edinburgh, Leyden or Heidelberg rather than Oxford or Cambridge. Doctors practising in the London area had to belong to the Royal College (from 1518), which printed lists of members, and there are biographies of the senior ones in *Munk's Roll*.

Surgeons are not so well covered. Surgery was a sideline of barbers, and London ones were members of the Barber-Surgeons Company. In 1745, they divided and there were surgeon-apprentices, who may be found in hospital records. They will appear in local directories, and all are listed from 1845.

Many doctors were apothecaries (with a London Company of their own from 1617). There are apprentice records from 1670 at the Guildhall Library. The qualification of Licentiate of the Society (LSA) was held by many early doctors, rather than MD.

Lawyers

Law Lists, of barristers and solicitors, have been printed from 1775. Earlier barristers appear in *Registers of the Inns of Court* mainly from 1500. Solicitors might attend one of the lesser Inns or be apprenticed as articled clerks to practising solicitors, and there should be records from 1729 at the PRO.

Provincial solicitors and their clerks handled local wills, and their signatures and career progress, from clerk to partner, can be traced in these and in any local directories. Surviving firms may have records of their early days – the problem is to discover the current name of the firm, which would have changed up to late Victorian times, since when names of long defunct partners may have been retained.

Men of Property

Most families will have owned a certain amount of property at some time. Primogeniture ensured that most real estate went to the eldest son, whose descendants would tend to be richer than those of his younger siblings. Second cousins could be 'poor relations' but mentioned in the will of a rich man. Inevitably, there are more classes of documents which will help locate the better off, but even a tiny amount of property will qualify, especially where taxes are being levied.

Owning one acre was the qualification for listing in the *Modern Domesday* of 1875 (see it at the library). There are numerous earlier lists which fix the residence of a person in a particular place in that year. Most of them are concerned with taxation in some way, and are mainly either at the CRO or the PRO. Most list landlords or householders only, though Poll Tax lists include others in the family.

Specialised levies, like the Hearth Tax (1662–74), Scottish Hearth Money (1690–93) and Window Tax (1696–1851) give a clue to the size of the house, and the Hair Powder Tax (1795) to the fashionable habits of the owner, therefore to social status. Others, like the so-called 'voluntary contributions' of Stuart times, Ship Money, and sundry odd subsidies, survive patchily, and some returns have been printed. The CRO should know what is available for your county, or see the lists in *Hearth Tax and other late Stuart Taxes* (Gibson).

A Protestation Oath was required in 1642, for men of 18 plus to sign accepting the Protestant religion (Gibson guide). Two Oaths of Allegiance were demanded, in 1689 and 1722, and an Association Oath in 1695, swearing loyalty to the monarch, from all owners of an acre or more, so that some women are included. In 1722, Quakers were allowed to affirm, so their religion is shown. By no means all these lists survive and where they do, it is mostly in association with the Clerk of the Peace's records.

Land Tax records (1692 onwards to 1950) show owners, tenants of the larger farms or cottages and the amount paid, but in general, the property is only described as 'house and land', unless it is unusual, like a mill or inn. If your ancestor appears as a tenant, the will of the owner may be informative. The tax record shows, very approximately, when deaths occur. Very few Land Tax records survive before the mid 18th century. A complete list is printed in the Gibson series.

The right to vote was based on a property qualification, varying from time to time, but in rural areas based on the '40 shilling freeholder' level, which was substantial, and later the £10 tenant. In towns, the right to vote could be more widely spread, partly because the buildings were worth more, and might include most householders with a fireplace. Poll Books showing not only who could vote but how they voted were printed regularly. Details of what survives are listed in two Gibson guides to *Poll Books* and *Electoral Registers*.

At any stage, having sons in a craft trade implies the possession of money or property by the father. Wills are an obvious source, if you know the father's name. Some craftsmen moved during or after apprenticeship, but their father's name may appear in apprentice records.

Anyone intending to trade in London had to prove apprenticeship. The Livery Companies therefore kept records of their own incomers, with details of parentage and even baptismal certificates appended. If the admission was 'by patrimony', then the father or another relative was also a member. If someone is referred to as a Citizen (and Grocer/Goldsmith/Tallow Chandler etc), he was a Freeman of London and will be recorded in the City Chamberlain's office, Guildhall, London EC2P 2EJ (from 1681).

Corporate towns also kept a Burgess Roll of Freemen, and there should be associated Apprentice Rolls, stating the father's name, residence, master, trade and cost of apprenticeship. Normally, a boy was 14 when indentured for seven years, though some were younger, especially in sea-going trades, and before about 1750. Only richer persons' sons could be apprenticed to the luxury trades, like goldsmith, embroiderer, mercer etc.

From 1710, a tax was levied on apprenticeships, and a central register was kept till 1808 (at PRO). There is an index at the Society of Genealogists and Guildhall Libraries to these, up to 1774, giving details as above till 1760 but no father's name after that. Boys apprenticed for small sums to relatives are excluded, which is a pity.

Pauper children, especially orphans, were apprenticed by the parish and these records may be found with other overseers' papers at the CRO. They were not taxed. Private apprentices in rural areas or outside the taxed period are unlikely to have surviving records, unless in family hands.

Manorial Records

In most cases, property passes by will, but the earlier ones do not necessarily mention some types of land which pass from father to son by other means.

A high proportion of property in England at one time was held as part of a manor. There may be more than one manor in any village, some very small, and perhaps part of a larger estate owned by a gentleman who lived elsewhere. Ask the County Record Office if they have the manorial records for the manor(s) in your village or if not, where they are. The point is that records tend to be deposited where the owner lives at the time, and this may be long after his family have lived on or actually sold up parts of their estates. Failing this, do a bit of digging.

The simplest way to ascertain what the local manors were and the descent of ownership, is to read the *Victoria County History*, if one has been compiled. Although it is by no means infallible about the smaller manors, and often has great gaps in descent, the name of the last owner, probably early in this century, will be shown. In the absence of a 'VCH', there may be an individual county history or even a local history. If you know the name of the manor, and a likely owner, you can consult the Historical Manuscripts Commission, Quality Court, Chancery Lane, London WC2, who have compiled a list of such documents and their whereabouts. They do not keep actual records there, so write first.

Much land, especially small lots, was held 'by copy of court roll' from the lord of the manor, a kind of perpetual and heritable tenancy, with power to sell or mortgage, by tacit agreement with the lord, and subject to payment of rent in cash or kind, and small sums of money on each transfer.

Manor court rolls or books show the transactions in this copyhold property. The first entry may be a report of the death of the tenant/father between two stated court dates, and the name and relationship of his heir, with his age if under 21. Then will come the admission of the heir, giving a detailed description of the holding, and where the land lies exactly in the fields, plus the date when the father himself was admitted, and the tenant previous to that. This leads you, in a simple case, to the next generation back, and the date of admission of the grandfather, and so on.

The process may be varied by a surrender before death into the hands of two other tenants, who are supposed to get the paperwork for the transfer completed. Sometimes the surrender states that the tenant and his wife are to hold the land for life, and only after the death of the survivor is the son to get it. If the tenant wishes to hand over his copyhold to other than his eldest son, or to divide a larger holding of bought-in land, then an abstract of his will may be included.

In a few instances, inheritance passes to the youngest son not the eldest (Borough English) or is subdivided between all sons (gavelkind). If male heirs fail, then the property will usually go to the daughters, usually jointly, sometimes to the eldest, according to the custom of the particular manor. The husbands are admitted (jointly with their wives) and the copyhold should pass to children of this marriage only, not a second marriage of his. If reference is made to admission to a 'moiety' (half) or 'fourth' then this could be a share passed through daughters of an original tenant.

Many tenancies are chequered by conditional surrenders, meaning mortgages to raise a cash sum. If the sum plus interest is paid by a certain date, the surrender is cancelled, if not, the borrower is in penalty for twice the amount and may have to take another mortgage to pay the first one. This can be resolved by the proceeds of a good harvest, or result in the loss of the copyhold to the mortgagee. This accounts for a farmer of 1780 leaving no will in 1790.

Sometimes manorial court books are incomplete, though there may be an alternative cash book, the Fine and Heriot Book, stating when X was admitted and what he paid as fine (final payment) for whose property. The heriot is a sum of money or equivalent in kind ('an ould horse') paid on transfer or disposal of all the property by the tenant. Most court and fine books were indexed, to help the steward of the manor check who had paid what when. Fuller details are in *Manorial Records* (McLaughlin).

Books before 1733 were written in Latin, though if you get to grips with the odd phraseology of post-1733 entries, you will probably be able to work out roughly what they were getting at before that. Will extracts and many of the place names are in English. Personal names and relationships are Latinised. These will be found in *Simple Latin* and examples of documents and a glossary of terms in *Manorial Records*. For medieval work, Denis Stuart's *Latin for Local and Family Historians* is recommended.

Other small holders of property may be more difficult to trace. If they retained the property, they should leave a will. The awkward ones are those who prospered for years but lost money just before their deaths.

Deeds

Private transactions of sale or long lease would in general result in a deed, with an indentured copy in the hand of the buyer, the seller and probably a draft with the solicitor arranging it. An indenture is a signed parchment with one wavy edge, originally written twice, head to tail, and cut across the middle, so that the two halves can be matched if necessary to prevent fraud.

Many solicitors have held deeds in safe keeping for clients long defunct, or acquired them as 'spares' at a later transfer, since only an abstract of title before 1920 is legally required for house deeds now. Some solicitors have deposited extensive collections with the CRO or other local repository, and it is always worth asking. Some, unfortunately, have destroyed all the old deeds in the interests of space in the office.

Leases

Apart from freehold purchase, much property was held on lease, sometimes for the fixed term of 7, 10, 20, 30, 50, 99, 199 or even 999 years. Apart from the last, the lessor does expect them to revert to himself or his family in due course, in good repair. This may leave a farming family suddenly without a home, after two or three generations.

In some areas, the fixed lease was uncommon. In the West Country, in particular, much property was held on the 'lease of lives' system. The lessee names three persons, normally including himself, during whose collective lifetimes the property was to stay in his family. He could select anyone, family or not, but would generally choose two young members of his own kin: not infants, because so many died, but sturdy children were preferred. If one died, it was generally permitted to substitute one name, on the payment of a further moderate sum. Occasionally, two or even more substitutions were agreed, where the original owner was more strapped for cash than provident for the distant future. The original lease and the substitutions often give details of relationships and deaths of persons in three or more generations. CROs may have these leases of lives, where the vendor was an institution or an owner of a large estate.

Estate papers

Many leases (and some freehold purchases) were made by individuals from large local landowners. There may be a record of a series of such transactions, going back for several generations, among estate papers of the landowner concerned. Many of these have now been deposited, with the same proviso as for manorial rolls above – they are likely to be in the county where the family have their main home, or where they lived when they decided to hand over.

Where members of the family are known to have worked for local gentry families, their estate records may provide useful additional information. They may include wage books for servants, details of their work, and occasionally personal notes on their engagement. There may be references in family letters or diaries deposited. Knowing where the other estates of gentry were is valuable in locating the possible origins of their servants. Personal maids, footmen and cooks were often imported. Gamekeepers were regularly brought in from a distant area, so that they should not be too friendly with the locals. So were farm bailiffs (Scots and northerners were very popular), for the same reason.

Land registration

As a compulsory feature, for purchases of freehold property, this came late to most areas, but there were Registers of Enrolled Deeds in Middlesex from 1702 and Yorkshire (held at Wakefield) from about 1720. Both have indexes of the vendors' names. Conveyances of freehold land could be enrolled in local courts. These are sometimes found in CROs among the Clerk of Peace records. More often, prominent families exercised this option to register these 'deeds of bargain and sale' in Chancery Close Rolls, Exchequer Rolls and Placita (Plea) Rolls of the courts of law. Some have been printed. The Scottish Sasine Rolls date from 1617 and the more general Register of Deeds from 1554. The Register of Deeds for Ireland is particularly useful in replacing lost alternative records.

The gentry

Most gentry families are well documented. *Burke's* or *Cockayne's Peerage* for those with titles, and *Burke's Landed Gentry* for the armigerous commoners are the best sources for these (Debrett is of limited use). As the qualification for being a 'landed' gent was 1,000 acres, it was far easier to achieve this in Ireland, hence the admission of a high proportion of Anglo-Irish families. This is useful, as many Irish records are missing, and families who lost their estates in this century may find previous generations well recorded.

Apart from national gentry listings, most counties have their own, including those with somewhat smaller land-holdings. First come the *Heralds' Visitations*, which are pedigrees of armigerous families, assembled and maintained by the College of Heralds, who would send someone round every 20 years or so to collect additions to existing families or new gentry details. The period covered is mainly the 16th and 17th centuries, and the details are only as reliable as the person providing them. Some 'new men' cooked up a pedigree from Adam or even Woden, and the heralds were not paid to argue. Some indeed were known to have taken bribes to help provide an impressive ancestry for an Elizabethan Johnny-come-lately. Most of these Visitations have been printed by the Harleian Society, and may show genuine evidence of an early gentry family which ceased to use arms in the 1600s, after dramatic losses in the Civil War.

Later 'county genealogies' were compiled at various dates by local historians, and detail what they know of former gentry families or, more often, what they are told of current ones, whom they hope will buy the book. Victorian new-rich also liked fictitious links with crusaders or foreign noblemen – the further away, the less easily checkable.

Berry and Walford covered a number of counties in Victorian times, the heyday of 'cover it over quick' genealogy, and should be treated with caution. Northern mill owners were often prouder of having beat their way up from near the bottom, so that some of their genealogies printed in *Foster's Familium Minorium Gentium* are more accurate.

There are also sometimes more critical pedigrees of families, discussed and printed in magazines like *Miscellanea Heraldica et Genealogica*, *Notes and Queries*, or the *Transactions* of County Record Societies or even Archaeological societies, once more interested in family history than they are now. The way to find any such references to printed pedigrees of families is via four books (listed in the bibliography) – Marshall's *Genealogists' Guide* and complementary volumes by Whitmore, Barrow and Thompson, normally filed together in a good reference library. They tell you the book, volume and page where the pedigree is to be found, and you can then consult it. Some of the books are very rare, and take some while to locate. Most would be in the Guildhall Library, or that of the Society of Genealogists. Many libraries now have Fax, which enables them to obtain a copy of a page for you, in quite a short time – or you can order the book through the Central Lending system which may take some weeks.

HOW MUCH FURTHER?

The Tudors and Before

Before parish registers, which may go back to 1538, and wills, some of which extend to the late 1400s, what can you find out about your family? Not a lot unless they are propertied in some way or are criminals.

If manorial rolls exist, there is possibly quite a lot about the descent from father to son or other heir and even some of the misdemeanours which ancestors committed.

Other freehold property transactions are well covered by the Feet of Fines, which are summaries of final agreements concerning sales, transfers, dowries, entails and other dispositions. Sometimes a couple and their eldest son will be named, sometimes reversions to brothers etc are mentioned. Fines for at least 17 counties have been printed, mostly for the 12th to 14th centuries, though Cambridge entries to the reign of Elizabeth I are published.

Because the church owned so much land, the cartularies of abbeys also contain a great many transactions, and a number of these have been published. The County Record Office and/or County Reference Library should know about this and have copies of the books. All the above records were kept in Latin, and not every editor has had the sense to translate them, but an English summary is generally given.

Although non-propertied people are not generally mentioned, some may be listed as tenants of the land in question, or sign as witnesses of a monastic transaction.

Tenants in chief from 1235 to 1660 had an Inquisition Post Mortem taken on death. This stated the date of death, what the person had owned, and who the heir was. If the heir was under 21, the age was stated and the name of anyone taking revenues reported. The land description is useful for connecting different generations.

Taxation lists. These are a valuable source of names, showing that a particular person lived in a certain place on a certain date and had at least a small amount of land or goods. The Subsidy Rolls have an obvious use, but do not neglect the Musters Rolls. Ostensibly, they are lists of weapon owners and men ready to serve in defence of the country, but they also include men liable to finance the militia, and their property values. The 1522 'Musters Roll' was a disguised tax assessment device, followed by the collection on a subsidy in 1524 on the declared property values.

Tax lists from the 13th and early 14th centuries survive (in the PRO) and a number have been printed by national or local bodies. These earlier lists may be simple ones of name plus tax paid, which gives some idea of status; or fuller entries of the possessions on which X was to be taxed.

David Stevens had 1 beast 2s, 1 steer 4s, 1 qr wheat 3s 4d, ½ qr beans 16d, hay and fodder 12d, sum 11s 8d, the fifteenth (tax) 9½d (Quainton, Bucks 1332).

The snag is that not all surnames were inherited from this period. David has a surname (son of Steven) but his son could be Davis. His contemporary, John le Cowherd might have descendants called Coward, or Johnson, or Mursley (his home) or Carpenter, Redhead, etc. And Walter Redhead's brown-haired sons could be named Walters, or Watkins. Proof of continuity of a name in one family is only possible if the same property descends from one generation to the next. There are nasty gaps in many records during the 14th or 15th centuries which spoil this proof.

A similar type of information may be obtained from court records. The Justices in Eyre of the king heard cases all over the country, ranging from murder and rape to property disputes. Participants in cases will be described by their parentage and often bring a relative to court to support their pleas, and interesting 'slice of life' stories may be revealed. Sometimes in land cases a complex section of pedigree over three or more generations may be presented. However, the problem again is one of changing surnames, which muddy the descent to later times.

Some families were habitually litigious. With luck, they will engage in disputes which were brought to the Chancery Court for settlement from about 1400. Some at least of the paperwork connected with these has been preserved at the PRO and if a case can be located, it is often excellent value genealogically. Even witnesses may state ages, birthplaces, past careers, relationships to the main parties, and so on. The difficulty is to find the case, for the official index is to plaintiffs only. Charles Bernau has indexed many of the other litigants involved and part of the period 1613–1713 has a published index, but there are many treasures yet to be uncovered. As the oldest inhabitants were often called to give evidence, any case involving persons from your ancestral village may be a gold mine.

LAYING OUT A PEDIGREE

What do you want to achieve?

After you have collected a lot of family information and arrived at a reasonably definite version of your family's descent for a fair number of generations, you will want to be able to display the results of your work, if only to a limited audience. This is the point where you have to decide what effect you are after.

Do you want to display all you know about the recent family, in a reasonably complete and legible form, so that others can read and understand it? Do you want to pack everything in, and amaze the natives by the amount you know and the hard work that must have gone into it, without caring so much whether they can understand it? Do you want to select part of the information only, to show what is relevant to a particular branch of the family, as a gift for them, or a wall decoration for yourself?

There are no laws which say that the only way of laying out a pedigree is thus, and any variation will brand you as a steaming amateur. Different forms are used for different purposes and the one which suits you is the one you are entitled to use. Any approach is valid, if it pleases you, but the methods of selection, organisation and layout are different – and the kinds of reproduction available too.

The truth, the whole truth . . .

The only criterion is that the pedigree should be as accurate as you can make it in the light of current knowledge, and that no guesswork should be shown as fact without a note to that effect. Once something is down in black and white, it tends to be believed – even by the person who wrote it down – so if in doubt, say so. A lot of pedigrees depend in places on educated guesses, or 99% certainties, especially interim pedigrees of half a dozen generations, done in the light of limited knowledge.

If honest doubt is admitted, then sooner or later, someone may stumble on the absolute proof, or the small piece of information which ruins the theory. Either way, you will want to know, and, unless you are completely arrogant, you would not want a claim to positive information in your pedigree to mislead someone else or, alternatively, make them think you are totally dishonest.

There is also the problem of publicising facts which will upset someone. If this can be avoided, then it is perfectly all right to omit the distressing detail, but not to falsify it. Victorians used to edit out any members of the family whose occupations were socially unacceptable. This is ridiculous now, when sensible people take pride in those who have overcome 'low' origins or adversity, and I would not tolerate editing demanded by snobbery. The standard of judgment is probably 'would any reasonable person of any age group think that was disgraceful?'

However, there are events which happened in every family which are regarded as less than admirable by most people – relatives are not keen to draw attention to a link with the Yorkshire Ripper or the Moors murderers. It is up to you whether you list the Christian name with no comment, or – if it is an uncommon one – conceal it as *one dau.* or *and other issue* in any selective pedigree produced while the name is hot news, provided that you somewhere have full information to pass on to less involved generations of the family.

There are still elderly people who would be bitterly embarrassed if the facts of illegitimacy, insanity or even divorce in their immediate family were revealed for others to see. It is tactful to find some formula for keeping such details unobtrusive or even omitting them from versions of the pedigree which will come into the hands of Auntie Flo or her family enemies and especially from those of her neighbours. Insanity is easy – *died 1936* is adequate without adding *in Colney Hatch Asylum*. Divorce may be coped with by omitting the death date of the first wife, if it is vital to include a second marriage. After all, you might not have known when she died. Illegitimacy is trickier, and this is discussed later. Always have a correct version of the pedigree, but don't flaunt it where it would cause mental and maybe physical distress to the old and vulnerable.

Computer generated pedigrees

There are many programs on the market which will take your data, sort it and lay it out for you according to a set pattern. If you have a good look at the results first and make sure that it will suit you, then all (!) you have to do is follow the instructions. However, if you want to control your own layouts, make a calligraphic pedigree for display, or even decide what to feed into the maw of the computer, the following pages will help you.

The line pedigree

This is the 'ordinary' set out pedigree, dealing normally with a single family surname. The whole system is formed from combinations of basic family units. The marriage of John Brown to Mary Smith and the list of their children, Ann, Betty, Charles, Donald, Emma, and Fanny is shown at its simplest as follows:

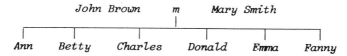

The husband's name is on the left of the paper, the wife's on the right, linked by *m* for married. Some people use '=' instead, but this leaves you stuck for an adequate sign to express other unions which produce children – and there are a lot of them about. Older genealogists either left them out, which misses some stable families and known cousins, or faked a marriage, which is misleading. A single line '-' for irregular unions looks like a dash or slip of the pen. From the marriage symbol comes a line of descent, which spreads out horizontally to accommodate the names of all their children, ideally set out equally on each side of the *m* symbol, if they were considerate enough to have an even number. As far as possible, the descent line to each child should be central to his or her name. This is a counsel of perfection, achieved only in the simplest cases. The children's names appear in chronological order, unless for special reasons discussed below. Some old pedigrees list all the males first, then the females, largely because in peerage families, daughters are irrelevant until all the sons die out. There is no excuse for this now, since it confuses the reader and falsifies the state of the family.

If John married twice, then he is flanked by his two wives, in order, and the descent line runs from each marriage symbol to their own group of children.

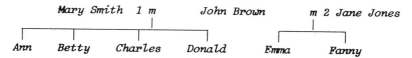

If there were three marriages with children, then the second wife appears centrally, under the name of the husband, which still allows the children to be set out in chronological order.

```
Mary Smith 1 m        John Brown      m 3 Alice Green
           |        m 2 Jane Jones        |
           |                              
```

The symbol ↑ shows that there were children, not here named. This will be used a lot in complex pedigrees.

The numeral is on the far side of the marriage symbol from the person to whom it applies.

If one of the wives produced no children (*d.s.p.*), place her marriage and name above that of a productive wife, in the right order if possible.

Mary Smith 1 m   *John Brown*   *m 2 Jane Jones*
                                                        d.s.p
                                                m 3 Alice Green

If a man marries four times, then the old way of doing things sometimes produced a strange effect.

John B   m 1 Mary S m 2 Jane J m 3 Alice G m 4 Anna T

This confuses and could shock a maiden aunt who thinks it shows the onset of the permissive society. The way to cope with this is either to extend the detailed entry referring to the husband into a broad, shallow box to which the ladies' names are appended horizontally at intervals:

John Theophilus Brown D.D., M.A.
1801 – 1897
R. of Chumbleigh 1829-48; Dean of Plige 1849-60; Bp of Gorringe 1861-92
Mary S 1 m   m 2 Jane J   m 3 Alice G   m 4 Anna T

Or, with a less detailed entry, set out the first three as above, then repeat his name before the entry for the fourth wife.

Mary S 1 m John Brown m 3 Alice G

m 2 Jane J   *he m 4 Anna T*

If a woman marries more than once, the same principle can be followed, if it is intended to show her children on the pedigree. As a rule, children are shown under the name of the husband, so on this pedigree sheet any number of husbands can be listed vertically under the name of the lady, with or without an 'issue' symbol.

If John Brown died, and his widow married again, she may have been known to the grandchildren by that name, as *e.g. Granny Jones*, which could give a wrong impression of her daughter's maiden name. To cope with family arguments about the results of your researches, enter both names clearly.

If John married a widow, it is usual to include her maiden name, if known, and that of her first husband.

John Brown 2 m Mary Gray m 1 George Black

The married name, Black, is the one which will appear in parish register or certificate, when she marries John Brown, but the Gray family is the ancestral one to be followed. Read outwards from the person to establish which

marriage is which. The combination of signs and numbers copes with complicated multiple marriages.

Jane J 1 m John B 2 m 2 Mary G 3 m 1 George B m 2 Anna D

This is the shorthand form of what will appear in your family history as
*John Brown first married Jane Jones, . . . after whose death, he married Mary
daughter of Dr James Gray. She was the widow of George Black, whose third
wife she became after the death of Anna Doxy, an actress, notorious as the
mistress of the Earl of Cheltenham.* (This could be name-dropping for the sake
of it, but might be included to account for the possession by the family of a
painting of the lovely Anna.)

Similarly, it may be relevant to include in the ancestral family mention of a
son or daughter of a former or later husband of the mother of the family,
because he/she left an important legacy to your own kin.

```
John Verney 1 m    Mary Nicholson    m 2 Richard Calvert
       |                                    |
           Mary Verney           Catherine Calvert
       d unm leaving all          m Rev. R. Wright
        estates to sister        (took name Verney)
```

In pedigrees dealing with medieval or even later persons, there may be
doubt about which children belong to which wife. There is no guarantee that
the widow named in a will is the mother of all or any of the children, for
example. In this case, set the wives down in order, symmetrically, but stem
the line of descent from the husband only, not a marriage symbol.

Sibling problems

The names of children in the same generation should ideally be entered in the
same horizontal line in chronological order. This may be varied for good
reasons, and only if no confusion is caused. Where you are faced by a multiple
marrier whose first wife died in childbirth, followed by the infant, it may
make sense to tuck her and the baby in a couple of lines above the rest of the
family, especially if there are a lot of siblings to accommodate. (Sibling is a
convenient neuter word to cover brothers and sisters, though it should mean a
small gossip.)

When you are faced by the 'Victorian bulge', where large families in their
turn produced large families, you ought properly to use a sheet of paper large
enough to accommodate all the cousins in line abreast, like a thin black line of
soldiers advancing across the landscape. But many Victorian children died
young, and the excessive production of the period was followed by heavy
losses of men in the First World War and a marked natural recession of
numbers from the 1920s, when contraception became more generally known
and used. If you lash out and buy a large sheet of paper to cope with Victorian

excess, you will find yourself with a lot of white spaces at the bottom, unbalancing your tree and adding to the expense and problems of handling and display of the finished article.

There are devices for packing the cousins in tighter without losing clarity, especially where you know the names of a group from the census, but have only found what happened to a few. If you have a family of eight, of whom four died, or did not marry, then stagger the names.

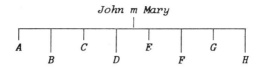

Think about it first and don't trap C in the upper rank if he is one whose family you want to follow. Leave the minimum amount of space for the 'top rank' children's details, but don't run these across the descent lines for the lower rank set, or these will look like grandchildren of John and Mary, instead of children.

If a couple had four children, all of whom died, then you can set them out in the normal way, but as close as possible to their parents' generation, leaving the space below to accommodate their adjacent cousins. This would fill a short, widish space. You could set them out one below the other, with brief details:

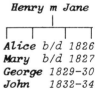

This saves lateral space but if your problem is vertical space, it won't help. Usually it is space, full stop. It goes against the grain to omit details it has taken months to get but, if you are really pushed, you could write:-

> *Henry m Jane*
> *2s 2d d. inf (two sons, two daughters, died as infants)*

or

> *d.s.p.s. (died without surviving children)*

One possible way of coping with the Victorian bulge is to write the names and issue of the older children of the family across the top of the sheet in the usual way, then to carry the drop line down the side and across beneath them. This tends to be confusing and is really only justified if the older branches, from *A, B, C*, practically die out (or your knowledge of them dies out and is likely to stay that way); or the younger branches, from *D, E, F*, take over all the momentum of the family from the others. If you descend from *F*, then this form of layout may suit you, since your main knowledge is likely to be of the younger branches.

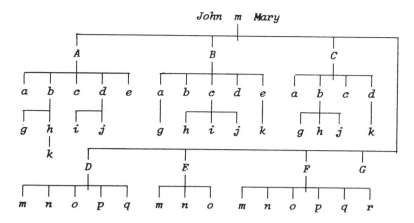

To make it totally clear what you are doing, thicken the line which connects all the children of the first generation $(A-G)$. Even so, it will still throw a lot of people, who think lower down the page must mean lower down the family. It is more justifiable in the earlier generations of the family, since you are less likely to meet one of the $a-k$ families. If you do this sort of trick with Victorians, you are bound to be confronted by new information about three generations of descent from a g or c which the proud cousins want inserted then and there.

So, you could get your large tablecloth, lay out all the known family upon it, trying it out first on lengths of old wallpaper or lining paper, then get the finished result photographically reduced to a manageable sheet, probably B4 or A3 size. If you have a lot of information, this will leave you with a pretty big sheet packed with small writing. Very impressive, but hard on the eyes and not readily taken in by anyone but an experienced genealogist. It is a useful thing to have to give the idea of the whole sweep of the family, and looks good skied on the wall, but for practical purposes of display + comprehension, you will need something smaller and/or simpler.

It may be better to break up the family into separate branches on separate A4 or B4 sheets. The latter give you more space, but the former size is about the largest which can be sent through the post without arriving crushed and battered. You could draft your tree on B4 and reduce to A4, remembering the comment about small writing and legibility. A lot of people you want to show the tree to will be elderly relatives, whose eyesight is not what it was.

The simplest division of the family above would be to put D to G on a separate sheet. Don't just run the line out from C to the side and start a second sheet with just the line and D to G pendant, with no parents, or even with *John* and *Mary* at the top and D as the apparent first child. Sooner or later, someone will lose the first sheet and it will appear that the only family they had was D, E, F and G. You could label each one who appears on a subsidiary sheet as *the 4th son* etc. This may work, but if there is more than one couple named John and Mary (and it happens often) then someone is sure to ask if that was the John and Mary who were parents of Arthur, or the grandparents of Cyril. If both of them had a fourth son named David, you will have to think fast.

A better jog to the memory is to head each sheet with *John m Mary*, and all their children's names listed (or if space is tight, the names of the sons, or a notable son). Only one or two of them will have full descents given on this sheet, but all the others have cross references made to the sheet where the full details of the other children and their descendants can be found. This is done by dropping a short descent line from the child whose branch is to be dealt with elsewhere and showing which sheet it is to be found on in a small box.

Decide what to call your sheets: *1, 2, 3* is possible and unlimited, but less practical than *A, B, C* or *Table A, Table B*, etc. This is partly because you may need to number the actual child in the family you are dealing with, and there are circumstances in which child *4* will not appear on sheet 4.

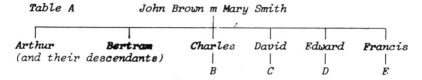

You may choose the chronological approach, and put all the descendants of the oldest son or sons on the first sheet, then start new sheets for each of the younger ones who actually produce offspring. Unmarried or non-productive children can be dealt with on their parents' sheet. Those with few children can share a sheet with another brother – especially if cousin marriage or legacies link the two.

Mostly, it depends on the size of each family. If Arthur had only two children, before dying young, and those children produced one child each, and no grandchildren, then they can well combine with Bertram, who had six children and eight grandchildren. Charles, who married twice and had ten children, needs a sheet of his own. David, with three wives and twenty children, needs several sub-sheets to get them all down.

Where there is not room on a single sheet for all the children of one of the sons, you make subordinate tables in the same way, which can be labelled *Ca, Cb, Cc* and so on. This is better than just continuing the alphabet, and calling the sheet which deals with David's fourth son (and his eight children) *F*. It ties these grandchildren to their progenitor on the first table, and makes relationships clear. (You can carry on down as *Cca, Ccbb* and so on, as you find out more.)

This may sound like a load of fuss-pottery, but it helps you to find your way around your records fast and without scrabbling through pages, which crumples your laboriously done fair copy, and ruins your reputation as the family expert. Even if you have a fair-sized family tree now, there will be more, and you need a flexible system which can add in cousin Bruce and his family from Australia when they contact you. The alphabet runs out amazingly fast if you lavish new letters on every new sheet. You can save up 'F' for the families stemming from a brother/cousin of John Brown, or for a different surname. Even if you haven't got that far yet, you will, and have to reletter all your trees or duplicate key names.

You may prefer to devote *Table A* to the details of your own line of the family, with the siblings relegated to secondary tables. This will presumably be the branch on which you have most information, down to the present day. Alternatively, you can exhaust the information about the first generation and follow the elder branches down till the page fills, and start your own line (from Charles, say) fresh on *Table B*.

Surname usage

It is conventional to use the surname for all males, but not for females. This may be impractical, but do always give a surname to the person at the top of your tree (even if the heading says which family it is) and to at least one male in each generation – ideally the one who is in direct ancestral line to you. It is often convenient to add a surname to someone with a short Christian name and three wives, or a long string of children, for the sake of balance. It isn't vital to use one for male children who died as infants. However, if a son is given a surname-forename, try to wedge in his family surname too, if possible, to avoid confusion. As multiple forenames always cause headaches in laying out the tree, you might have to reduce the actual surname to an initial. This never looks as good, and someone will always query it, but needs must at times.

What about the daughters?

Genealogy is a male-chauvinist sport, and strictly, the descendants of daughters should not appear on the Brown family chart, but on that of their husbands. In the list of the Brown siblings, full details of an unmarried daughter will appear on the main sheet or sheets; a married daughter has her Christian name with dates of birth and death, and the name of her husband underneath, and *d.s.p.*, if there was no issue. But if there were children, you should show a descent symbol and list them elsewhere. However, rules are made to be broken, and if what you know about the daughters' children is very limited but significant, and you have the space, put it in.

Otherwise, you could use a separate table for the descendants of the daughters, since you will need space to include the changed surname. It is important to differentiate between this surname and a surname used as forename. This can sometimes be accommodated neatly by tucking it in along the horizontal line of descent, above the children to whom it applies. Alternatively, write the surname in heavier lettering.

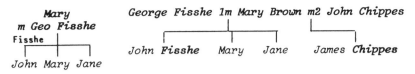

When one of the girls marries Archibald Fazakerley-Smythe, followed by Hildebrand Willoughby, you bless her sister who had one son, John, without marrying anyone.

Cousin marriages

Quite often, there were cousin marriages between the issue of brothers and sisters. Then you will certainly want to include the sister's child on the main pedigree, though there may not be room for the siblings. In this case, show the bride/groom and use a descent mark to show there were other issue not listed here. If a legacy came into the family through a relative on the female line, it may be possible to include this person too, for convenient reference when you are telling the family history.

Where a marriage between cousins unites the children of, say, the first and fourth brothers, then it is permissible to move brother four (*David*) out of chronological sequence, so that the two lines can be combined on the same sheet, but make it clear what you have done by marking the names with a superscript number to show the actual order.

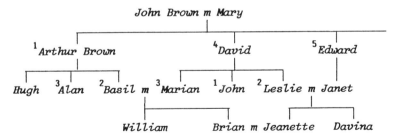

So far, so good, with not too many out of natural order. If John had children, they would have to be accommodated in another table, or the marriage details of Brian and Jeanette entered separately. Alternatively, Leslie and John could change places and the marriage of Leslie to Janet be entered in two places. The marriage date is repeated in both entries, but the dates of birth and death once only (unless there is ample space). Insert 'cs' (or cousin) and an arrow to show which direction to look further. If other considerations dictate that they appear on separate sheets, then if possible, repeat all dates. If not, use an arrow to indicate where to look.

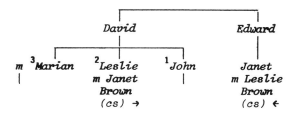

But if William also married Davina, there is no good way of juggling the order. I have seen two horizontal descent lines overlapped:

but even if this is done very carefully, with different colours for the two sets, it still confuses people, because Brian appears to be brother of the girls, and relatives of a nervous disposition may fear that they have incestuous triplets.

Normally, select which couple is more important to your tree, and set them together, leaving the other pair to their own devices. If one pair is childless, they are the ones to demote. Enter the marriage twice, as above. If both have children, choose the one in your direct line, or the one with the longest set of descendants, or the one most conveniently placed to have a deeper vertical entry on the page.

You may be hell-bent on showing that two brothers married two sisters, because it had a significant effect on the family history. A common occurrence was that pretty Miss Black attracted George, heir of Enoch White of Grindley, and her brother met and later married George's kid sister, Annie. In the fullness of time, George's daughter, Ena, married her cousin, Arthur Black, and all the lovely mills and money came to them. This was the making of the Black fortunes, and should certainly be recorded.

You could enter both spouses separately as *George son of Enoch White* and *Ann dau of Enoch White*, which doesn't make it totally clear that this is the same Enoch, unless you add repetitive detail. You could lengthen the drop line and tie the Whites together, with or without their father's name:

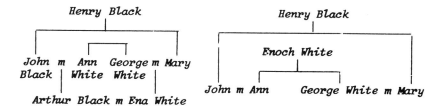

The snag about this is the amount of vertical space it may take, and the lack of room to include details of Enoch White, a key figure in the family history, who was older than Henry Black, not younger, as he looks to be here.

This is probably one of the few justifications for line crossing. If Enoch is set level with Henry, a few details can be included here, as well as on the White sheet, and the inheritance is explained. Cross the line with a definite double bend, squared or curved, to make the lines of descent quite clear.

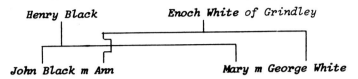

You might indicate the crossing point with a dotted tunnel (like a pipe work diagram) but this might be taken to indicate an illegitimate connection (see below).

In long Victorian families generations often got out of step with ages. It would be perfectly possible for Arthur to be grown up before Edward arrived, after a number of daughters/infant deaths not shown. If Arthur married early and Edward slightly late, then Janet could be the same age as Brian, though of the same generation as his father, Basil. A marriage between them would be legal and showing it would involve a lot of juggling and a very long vertical from Edward. There might be circumstances where it would be feasible – if everyone in between died off, struck down by plague or the 1919 flu, but on the whole this would be another case for showing separate details with arrows to link the names.

Never move part of the family if it doesn't improve the position as regards space and clarity, just to show what a clever clogs you are. Fidget the names around for best fit, and establish which are the most important lines to emphasise. On the whole, unless it is a simple matter, don't juggle the order too far, if it involves great lines swooping across the sheet.

Illegitimacy

Illegitimate children are shown with a line of descent from both parents, if known, or from the mother alone. The couple may be linked by an '=', or, if they later married, an *m*. The bastard child can be shown with a dotted or dashed line and the surname by which he is commonly known.

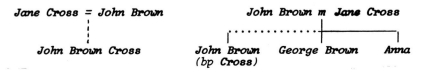

In the second entry, John was born before the marriage of the parents and known for a year or so by his mother's surname, but later they married and he dropped Cross to be known by courtesy as Brown.

However, most genealogists like to use a dotted or dashed line for cases where a relationship is pretty sure but not yet absolutely proved. It should be broken by a question mark, but is not always.

This indicates that the two men were born in the same place, close together, there were no other Punters in the area, they had the same occupation, but so far no baptisms or wills have turned up to clinch the relationship.

If the dotted line is used for hypothesis, then people tend to use a vertical line of dashes cut by a diagonal bar to show illegitimacy. This is probably intended as the 'bar sinister', a mark sometimes used on a heraldic shield where the father's arms were used by a bastard son.

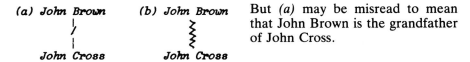

But *(a)* may be misread to mean that John Brown is the grandfather of John Cross.

If you don't want to use dots or dashes, a neat zigzag line *(b)* is preferable. Using a word processor keyboard, a lot of symbols are available which might be used.

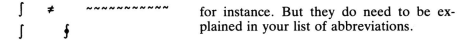

for instance. But they do need to be explained in your list of abbreviations.

Twin births

Twins are shown by branching a single descent line – but as they often died, they may be written in a block, one above the other with bracketed names, *b/d 1832.* You will occasionally get one live, one stillborn child. If there is space, note this (+ *dau. stillb.*), since knowing that there were twins in the family may be important to an expectant couple as the tendency is hereditary.

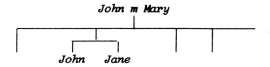

How much detail?

There is not much space in a line pedigree (except a two-three generation one) for a lot of detail. The place for this is on your record cards, note books or computer print out – and if possible, in your head as well, to trot out when someone asks a question about the tree. However, without any information of dates, places and occupations, it lacks something in use and interest. Give at least the year dates, the main occupations and locations – not every street address, but the main home(s) in adult life. The description of the person should include any name in normal use which is not a baptismal name, if this is how the family knew him or her.

Mary Ann (Polly)

Theophilus (Philip)

but not baby names:

Thomas (Snookums).

If the person habitually used the second or third of a string of names, write the disused ones small or bracket them off.

Where a man acquired a title or professional rank as an adult, add this in brackets too, or simply if it was a long term thing.

eg *(Sir) Henry Jones – knighted two years before he died,* or *Rev. Charles Smith – known as such from 23 to 89, and married to your great aunt under that description.*

Peerage titles should be given, with date of grant or succession, but include the surname or subordinate title if that was how the man was known for a substantial portion of his life. Changes of surname should be noted, with the date bracketed:

Thomas Sneyd (1815) -Kynnersley = became Sneyd-Kynnersley

James Brown (1891) Smythe-B = became Smythe-Browne

John Otway (1830) Barrett = born Otway, became J.O. Barrett

Otto (Maulstock) (1914) Marshall = dropped Maulstock entirely.

Try to keep all the information about a person under his name, or projecting evenly on either side.

John Smith *1824–1901* *Headmaster, South* *Kandapore College*	which can reduce to	*John Smith* *1824–1901* *Headmaster Sth* *Kandapore Coll.*

There is no point in reducing *Headmaster* to *Headmr* or *Hdmr*, or *South* to *S.*, because of the irreducible bulk of *Kandapore*. Be sure you are clear – *S.* in other entries could be *Saint* not *South*. Any description or place which occurs frequently can be shortened after the first time, or if a key is provided. A lot can be fitted into a small space if smaller size printing is used for the personal details, but make sure it is clear, and don't cut down the original size too far if you intend to have the result photographically reduced.

Most families have the same Christian name repeated in different generations. If one bearer of the name has been or done anything worthy of note,
consider labelling him, for your own sake as much as the reader's:

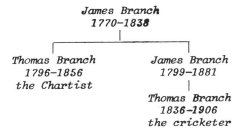

It staves off those repeated 'which
was the one who . . .' questions – or
at least it makes sure you point out
the right one first go.

Trial runs and experimental layouts

There is no denying the impressive effect of a complete family tree on a single
sheet (which can be backed up by dissected sections as outlined above). Large
paper is expensive, in the quality which you will need for a permanent record,
so get the layout right on cheaper stuff before you commit pen to final paper.
Lining paper, dog-ends of rolls of non-embossed wallpaper, sheets of computer paper stuck together, chip shop wrapping paper (pre-use) will accommodate even large Victorian families, and it isn't a disaster if you leave out all of
Uncle Fred's lot and have to start again.

Until you get to the Victorian bulge, aim to start with the eldest child and
exhaust all his descendants, even unto the fourth or fifth generation, then see
where the second child comes. If you write out a neat line of children of the
first generation, at regular intervals, then start on the second row, you won't
have enough room for the families of some, and too much for others. If space
gets very tight, you may have to move all the unmarried children into the gap
between George (who had twelve children) and James (who had fourteen),
rather than huddling them all together at the end of the line. It is a bit
misleading, so be sure you number them in their family order.

Try as far as possible to keep the details of someone's descendants
underneath their own name (so don't place number one son right over to the
left hand side of the paper) and, where it can be achieved, equally projecting
on each side, with a clear line stemming from the marriage symbol. Don't
place a parent too far over to the left, above someone else's children, and run
out a horizontal line parallel with one or even two others. This is confusing to
the eye. As far as possible, keep members of one generation on the same line,
but break the rule to get rid of small families with no next generation to
follow. This leaves room for their more productive siblings.

If it does happen you have masses of cousins to accommodate in limited
space for two generations, then all but one line dwindles and dies out, then it
would be permissible to run a straight descent line down from that sibling,

past the serried ranks of nephews and great nephews, and then spread his own family out in the empty wastes revealed below. As this is likely to be your own line of ancestry, this is effective and pleasing to the ego. Thicken the descent line – if it is central to the family, it looks like a tree trunk, or a diagram of the blood stream, with your kin as the main artery.

Write names in fairly even script, though if you are faced by Araminta Sophonisba Mariana, born and died within three days in 1825 (and not surprisingly, with a name like that) you may use smaller print for her. If you are very pressed for space, consider losing some of the short lived babies – + *3 daus d. inf.* may cover it. If you have a set of cousin marriages to fit in, work out that bit on a separate sheet and then copy it in. In fact, once you have got a section perfect, you could cut that bit out and stick it in place when you are redrawing the rough for the fourth time.

If your writing is not your best feature, you could type the names – but it is surprisingly difficult to lay out a typed tree, though word-processors or electronic typewriters make it easier to correct and jiggle about. The letters, if typed, should be proportionally spaced, but subtle adjustments are very much easier in handwritten work. Details of dates, occupations and locations can be written smaller than the names, and, if you like, each person's entry enclosed in a box. This looks nice but can be a bit inflexible when space is tight. Try to write most of the entry with parallel sides, or centred right and left. Irregularly framed entries were used in old pedigrees – these fit old style writing but are difficult to do neatly with plain modern script and look pretty horrible with typing. Olde worlde writing throughout is not really the solution – it doesn't read clearly.

At this stage, check all your dates for accuracy, and make sure you have not left out a whole generation, misled by repeated Christian names. Do your final check in the morning when you are fresh. If you happen to have a relative with an informed interest, get them to check over the tree. It is amazing what errors can creep past you late at night.

If you have done a lot of alterations or cut and paste work, make a final fair copy of the draft – it may seem a waste of time, but it does give an idea of how it will really look, and it may show up last minute imperfections – half inch adjustments may be needed or further abbreviations may help.

Leave room at the top for a heading (**'The Browns of Bagworthy'**) and at the bottom for imminent births or marriages – you can score a lot of Brownie points by adding the infant Emma or Shane before the eyes of the proud parents, in the space carefully left – but a squashed in extra can ruin a handsome pedigree.

The final layout

Measure up the exact size of paper needed and get it from an art shop, drawing office supplies shop or printer if necessary. Cartridge paper, or, ideally, thin drawing board, is not cheap, but this is a work of art you are producing. Sticking tacky little sheets of A4 together with tape is a waste of time – it will never look good, and the edges will show up if you have it reduced. Use Indian ink and steel pen, or an artists' lettering pen (try it out first, they take some getting used to). Biro or felt tip will not do.

If you are supremely confident of your calligraphic abilities, and have done pedigrees before, you could do a really special tree on parchment. This costs about £25/£30 for a skin the size of a small sheep, and you have to allow for natural shape and imperfections. Well done, it looks superb, but the nervous strain is immense. If you really want to do this, one of the few places in England where parchment is still made is the Cowley Works, Caldecot Road, Newport Pagnell, and they offer expert advice on how to do it (and make minor corrections).

A compromise is the parchmentised or textured paper sold in art shops – not the simplest thing to work on either. Pale tinted drawing paper is possible – always with black lettering for clarity. If you must use coloured ink or paint, limit it to one gorgeous splash, not a psychedelic splatter, which dazzles the eye and detracts from the effect of the tree.

Do resist the temptation to use fake olde Englishe lettering (except possibly for the heading). Some calligraphy classes teach this, but it is generally barely legible and frustrates those who try to read the pedigree. A good plain calligraphed script looks fine – there are several books and several classes on the subject. Neat script-style printing or writing, with judicious use of upper and lower case, can be tried out on the fair copy.

If you really can't write neatly, then Letraset is an attractive, though expensive, alternative. The smaller letters are more difficult to lay than the larger ones, and keeping a straight line does not come easily to us all. Probably fancy types are most used in pedigrees intended to be decorative rather than readable. If you are really desperate, you could take your fair copy to a calligrapher – don't ask them to lay a tree, though, which is the most time-consuming part of the work.

If you do embark on the Great Work, protect the lower part of your sheet with clean paper. Outlaw cups of coffee, chip butties, admiring neighbours, demanding infants, and, above all, cats, from the room. Take the phone off the hook and don't answer the door. Stop work as soon as you get tired (eyes, fingers, brain) and cover the sheet if you leave it even for a minute. It will take twice as long as you think, so don't start it the day before a birthday. When you make a small slip in the bottom line, as you will, treat it with typists' white-out, and don't hurl the whole lot in the fire in frustration. Remember, other people don't know what you meant to write, so leave out the death date for Auntie Flo if you have overrun the space for it, and cover a persistent blemish with a decorative curl if you can't obscure it. This is going to be something you and the family will be proud of, so it is worth taking trouble and time. Further details of other layout styles are given in the McLaughlin Guide (see Bibliography).

Useful abbreviations

(some to use, some to translate what you find in printed books)

b = born
m = married
d = died
bp = baptised
bur = buried
'=' can mean unmarried but having issue;
    often means married
unm = never married
b.b. = baseborn, illegitimate
nat.s = natural (bastard) son of
d. inf. = died as an infant/young
d. minor = died under 21
d. pre 1750 = died before 1750
d. post 1750 = died after 1750
fl. 1620 = was alive in 1620
c.1720 = roughly 1720
(fl.) temp. Hen VIII = (was alive) in the
    reign of Henry VIII
1980- or 1980+ = from 1980 and still is
gfr/gmr = grandfather/grandmother
ggfr = great-grandfather
3ggfr = great-great-great-grandfather
cos./cn = cousin
rel. = relative of
gdn = guardian
18c (or C18) = in the eighteenth century
    (*c.* = roughly, about)
'?', *quaere* = this information is unproven
    but quite probable
'??' = this may be so, but not very likely
(? *Burke*) = *Burke* doubts this
(*Burke* (?)) = I doubt *Burke*
W. = Will
W.d. = Will dated
W.pr. = Will proved
Admon/Adm = Administration
P.C.C. 1685 = proved 1685 in the
    Prerogative Court of Canterbury
P.C.C. *Pyne 233* = Proved in P.C.C. in
    the year named 'Pyne' (*i.e.* 1697). Each
    P.C.C. annual calendar used to be
    named after a prominent testator,
    rather than its date, and this 'code' may
    be met in older pedigrees.
W. Arch. Bucks. = proved in the
    Archdeaconry Court of Buckingham
yeo = yeoman
ag lab = agricultural labourer

1840+ = from 1840 till death or
    thereabouts

*All the following group with or without
    stops between:*

d.s.p./dsp = died without issue
    (*o.s.p. etc* in older forms)
d.s.p.m. = without male issue
d.s.p.s. = no surviving issue
d.s.p.l. = died without legitimate issue
d.v.p./d.v.m. = died in the lifetime of his
    father/mother
or any combination – e.g. dvpsplms
s John = son of John
dau/d Hugh = daughter of Hugh
s & h = son and heir of
coh. = joint heiress of
wid/widr = widow/er
rem. or m2 = remarried
div = divorced
mkr = maker
mfr = manufacturer
fwk = frame work knitter
-wrt = -wright
Cit. = Citizen of London (Freeman of a
    Livery Company)
Chmn = chairman
Pres = President
Ctte = committee
Cdr = Commander
Chw = churchwarden
D.L. = Deputy Lieutenant
Ll.D. = Doctor of Laws
Bp = Bishop
V = Vicar of
R = Rector of
Ven. = Venerable (*i.e.* Archdeacon)
v sub = see below
v sup(ra) = see above
q.v. = which see
cf = compare with
et al. = and others
sic = so (*i.e.* yes, really, however peculiar
    it looks)
i.u. or *iure ux(oris)* = (inherited) by the
    right of his wife

APPENDIX

Record Offices

A complete list of all Record Office addresses and location maps will be found in *Record Offices and How to Find Them* (Gibson). Some of them advise booking seats in advance, some demand it, and it makes sense to book first if you are travelling a long way to get there. Most of them are open 'office hours' Monday to Friday (some even less than that), but the better ones now have at least one regular extra period, either an evening or a Saturday morning, when documents ordered in advance can be seen by appointment.

Most Record Offices belong to the 'Archives Network' and require a Reader's Ticket for entry. This is because unscrupulous people have been pinching things, stealing or damaging irreplaceable heritage material which contains records of someone's ancestor – maybe YOURS. The tickets are free and easy to obtain if you produce evidence of identity – an official document with your name and address on, like a driving licence, pension book etc. Some offices also require passport photos – which make everyone look like a potential criminal – or a second, less often carried piece of identification, like a gas bill. If you write or phone in advance, they should tell you what the individual requirements are.

In general, Record Offices do not charge for research done in person. Gloucester and Devon do, at £2 a day or part; Hertfordshire charges higher fees (£2.50 for 4 hours or £4 a day) for use of any microforms, which includes parish registers. A few others charge a small sum for the use of bought-in microfiche material, which is possibly fair. These fees should be stated in advance and you should be warned if you need to book to use machines or films in heavy demand.

Most Record Offices are up or down flights of steps, and if this is a problem, enquire if access by lift can be arranged. Quite often it can, if they know in advance. Also check if you wish to use a laptop computer or take photos etc – some offices permit it, some just won't. The usual consideration is whether it will be a nuisance to other users. 'Noise pollution' is important when you are researching, and chatting into tape recorders is normally banned (and rightly so).

Take sufficient notebooks with you – tiny sheets the size of loo paper may look neat, but are soon overfilled and fit only for the above purpose. Allen & Todd of Ramsbottom have designed special packs of lined forms for almost all recording purposes. The alternative is either a collection of small notebooks (one for each purpose) or blocks of A4 paper which can be separated and filed in sets later.

Take a supply of pencils, since CROs do not allow ink or biro near original documents. 3B or 4B pencils make the darkest marks with least effort but need sharpening often. Take your own sharpener. CROs have them, but they either chew pencils up or fall to bits at the slightest provocation.

Most CROs want you to hand over cases and bags, even handbags in one instance, so put all the papers and pencils you need in a transparent envelope or zipped plastic wallet. Eat a hearty breakfast, so you don't need to stop at midday and hunt for a cafe unless you want to. Take a sandwich, but never eat in the search room, even sweets. Of course you can't smoke, and people who slip outside and come back reeking of it are none too popular.

Talk as little as possible, in a low voice if you need to ask someone. Folk who come in and pin the archivist to the wall with a blow by blow account of their fascinating ancestors or previous searches disturb the others and the atmosphere turns purple with unexpressed anger. Write to the CRO first, by all means, with a summary of what you have found that is relevant to their area, including occupations and saying what registers you wish to consult.

Ask if there are special sources they recommend peculiar to their office. They do rather expect that you will know enough to ask for the standard ones, rather than require a seminar on tracing your ancestors on the spot, but they should be able to say if someone has deposited a family tree, a diary or papers referring to your family surname; or has written/is writing a monograph about local glass-blowers, hemp-dressers or coffee-mill makers in your ancestral area, worth consulting for possible expert knowledge of your very own in that trade. Every CRO has a motley collection of manuscripts, maps and lists which might apply, and they know best what is available.

Draw a neat A4 size family tree of what you know already, with limited details, like the rough year date instead of full dates. If you have anything proved by certificate, write C in a circle against it; census ages can be given the year in a circle ⑤①. Remember dates from this source are approximate – even if they are totally accurate, they reflect age on that day only, and '26' in 1851 could lead to a birth date from March 31, 1824 to March 30, 1825. List the person as c1824/5 (and don't be surprised if he turns up in 1826 or 1823).

Work out a list of surnames you are searching for in this area because while you are about it, you might as well set down any Bloggs at all, and any of the names of direct female ancestors too, since they are part of the fabric. Although there is less point in noting all the names of families into which siblings or cousins marry, the actual person and his parentage may be useful.

For instance, if your grandfather's sister married Augustus Foljambe, and he was nephew of the local squire, it obviously makes a difference to the likely status and career prospects of the family.

Note down particular key Christian names and dates. If you know X-great grandma was Mary Porter, born in about 1796/7, then keep an eye open for Mary Porters born about then, noting their parents; then check if one has a brother William born about 1793/4, since he was living with the Bloggs in 1851. The marriage of the parents will bring in a new surname to research further back.

Write down and keep an eye open for witnesses to later weddings and 'visitors' in censuses. Quite a lot of them turn out to be relatives of some kind, or important clues to where your ancestor came from. If you write 'Mary Timmins 42 visitor 1861' or 'Henry Sprott wit. 1849' then you don't have to pause and try to remember if she was Simmons or he was Mott. But don't reject minor spelling variations out of hand. In those days, a lot of people were semi-literate at best and had to accept any spelling the parson or clerk dreamed up. If it sounds rite it is Wright.

Your aim is to gather up all the entries you can in the time available – don't stop to evaluate them apart from seizing the ones which match your 'key names' list as above. Make sure you head each sheet with the parish or source. Keep separate sheets for each source, then you can file them up when you get home. If you have to stop before you have completely searched a whole register, note the final date done; if it gets to five minutes from closing, and you skim over the next couple of years, note where you stopped being thorough.

Try to note the CRO reference number, especially if they find an unusual manuscript for you. You could find a register again, but the list of house-holders in Lady Mucke's charity records for 1802 isn't so easy. 'A little bundle of papers with pink tape round' won't do – they've got thousands of those.

Even if you search a register and find nothing, note BLOGGS nil. (Say exactly which names you have searched for, since when you discover a new name, the parish with no Bloggs may be stiff with Maynards.) You don't want to waste time doing exactly the same thing again six months later. Worse, some bright spark might suggest doing it for you, and charge for finding nothing. (But if you do hire a researcher, you would have to pay for a negative search, because it is the time taken which counts, not the amount found).

Family Historians' Law. The last ten minutes of the day will be the time you find the most important entry.

USEFUL ADDRESSES & BIBLIOGRAPHY

Family Records Centre, Myddelton St, off Rosebery Ave, London EC1R 1UW. Now holds all GRO indexes, censuses 1841-91 (from 2002, the 1901 census), nonconformist registers, PCC wills + selection of other records on microform. Open Mon-Sat 9-5, Tue (10am) and Thur to 7pm

Public Record Office, Ruskin Ave, Kew (army, navy, merchant navy, colonial, maps, tithe and enclosure awards, other modern records) open Mon-Sat as above; Readers ticket required, obtainable with ID.

Guildhall Library, Aldermanbury, London EC2P 2EJ (City of London R.O., directories, Lloyd's captain's registers, most books, lists and indexes, I.G.I. maps.) Mon–Sat, free access

Society of Genealogists' Library, 14 Charterhouse Buildings, Goswell Road, London EC1M 7BA (Tue–Sat; fee to non-members. T/S registers, censuses, many books, directories, indexes, lists, M/S pedigrees etc)

British Library Newspaper Library, Colindale Avenue, London W9 5HE (Mon–Sat)

Society of Friends Library, Friends House, Euston Road, NW1 2BJ (T/S Quaker registers, Minute Books, histories; fee)

(Methodist archives) John Rylands library, Deansgate, Manchester M3 3EH

Dr Williams's Library, 14 Gordon Square, London WC1H 0AG (many obituaries, chapel histories etc, but does NOT hold Dr Williams's Register (at PRO)

United Reformed Church History Society, 86 Tavistock Place, WC1H 9RT (records of Independent, Congregational etc churches, ministers)

Baptist Union, 4 Southampton Row WC1 (but most archives at Regent's Park College, Pusey Street, Oxford)

LDS (Mormon) Family History Centre, 64–68 Exhibition Rd, Kensington W7 (and all over the country)

County, City & Area Record Offices: addresses and locations are given in *Record Offices & How to Find Them (England + Wales)*
Greater London

Full details of London Borough Archives in *London Local Archives: A Directory of . . . Record Offices*

London Parish registers and copies; listed for Inner and Outer London, inc Nonconformist registers, from Society of Genealogists, who also have similar details for most counties in the *Parish Registers* series.

McLaughlin Guides (from SOG, PRO, Local FHSs, CROs, Family Tree Magazine or author, Varneys, Rudds Lane, Haddenham, Aylesbury, Bucks

HP17 8JP). *Starting your Family Tree; Interviewing Elderly Relatives; General Register Office indexes: 'Somerset House' (after 1858) wills; Wills Before 1858; Parish Registers; Illegitimacy; Annals of the Poor (to 1834); The Poor Are Always With Us (Victorian and after); Reading Old Handwriting; Simple Latin; Nonconformist Ancestors: Family History from Newspapers; Quarter Sessions; Manorial Records; Making the Most of the IGI; Laying out a Pedigree; No Time for Family History?; Surnames, origins and meaning.*

Gibson Guides (from FFHS, SOG, local FHS, FTM or author, Harts Cottage, Church Hanborough, Oxon). Location/dates of records *Simplified Guide to Probate Jurisdiction. Local Newspapers 1750–1920; Bishops' Transcripts + Marriage Licences; Electoral Registers; Census Returns on Microform (1841–91); Local Census Listings (early ones); Land Tax; Hearth Tax + Other Late Stuart Taxes; Quarter Sessions Records; Militia Lists; Victuallers' Records; Coroners' Records; Marriage & Census Indexes. Specialised Indexes; Poor Law Union records* (listed by area + general gazetteer)

Parish maps from Institute of Heraldic & Genealogical Studies, Northgate, Canterbury, Kent; also from CROs and area FH societies

In Search of Army Ancestry: Gerald Hamilton Edwards

Army Records for Family Historians: Simon Fowler (PRO)

Naval Records for Family Historians: N.A.M. Rodger (PRO)

My Ancestor was a Merchant Seaman: M.J. + C.T. Watts (SOG)

In Search of Scottish Ancestry: Gerald Hamilton Edwards

Tracing Your Irish Ancestors: Dominic F. Begley

Irish Roots Guide: Tony McCarthy

My Ancestor Was A Baptist: G. Breed (SOG)

My Ancestors were Congregationalists: D. Clifford (SOG)

My Ancestor was a Presbyterian/Unitarian: Alan Ruston (SOG)

My Ancestor was a Methodist: J. Brady (SOG)

My Ancestor was a Quaker: E. Milligan (SOG)

My Ancestors were Jewish: M. Gandy

My Ancestors were in the Salvation Army: R. Wiggins

My Grandfather was a Railwayman: T Richards

Register of One Name Studies: Guild of One Name Studies (SOG)

P.R.O. Leaflets on various records; e.g. Dockyards, Immigrants, Army, Navy, Royal Warrant Holders, Metropolitan Police etc., (available on-line)

Latin Glossary: J Morris

Latin for Local History: Eileen Gooder

Elizabethan Handwriting: 1500–1650: G. Dawson & L. Kennedy-Skipton (inc. facsimiles and transcripts)

Borthwick wallets 1. Mediaeval 2. Elizabethan 3. 17th century (similar facsimiles and transcripts) Borthwick Institute, University of York, Peaseholme Green, York.

Directories – Post Office, Kelly, Pigott, White etc

Transactions of the Huguenot Society (series, includes early registers)

Sources for Catholic & Jewish Ancestry (D. Steel)

Library consultation

Genealogists' Guide (G. Marshall 1903): *Genealogical Guide* (J. B. Whitmore 1903–53): *Genealogist's Guide* (G. Barrow 1975): *British Family Histories in Print* (T. Thompson 1980)

Burke's Peerage: Landed Gentry: Commoners: Vicissitudes of Families

Burke's General Armory (arms as used, many D-I-Y efforts)

Heraldic Families: Fox-Davies (guaranteed genuine)

Book of Crests: Fairbairn (as used, not all authentic)

Familium Minorum Gentium: Hunter (v. minor gentry, mainly northern)

Gentleman's Magazine (series)

Musgrave's Obituaries

Visitation pedigrees (Harleian Society)

Miscellanea Heraldica et Genealogica (large series)

Dictionary of National Biography (many volumes, strong on clergy)

Victoria County History (various counties, several volumes each)

Lists and Indexes

Prerogative Court of Canterbury Wills (Indexes 1700–1749 at PRO, available on microfiche; Indexes 1750–1799 printed, from SOG)

Harleian Society volumes (inc. parish registers etc)

Scottish Record Society volumes

British Record Society volumes

List and Index Society volumes

Phillimore's Marriage Registers (various counties)

National Index of Parish Registers: Details of church and chapel registers in most counties (SOG)

Cofresti Plywyf Cymru; Parish Registers of Wales (Williams)

Directories – Post Office, Kelly, Pigott, White etc

Professions and Trades

Alumni Oxonienses: Alumni Cantabrigienses (students at Oxford or Cambridge)

Index Ecclesiasticus: J. Foster (details of clergymen alive 1800–1830)

Clergy Lists: Crockford's Clerical Directory (from 1858)

Medical Register/Directories (from 1845)

University and School student registers (various, SOG)

Printed Poll Books; Electoral registers

Navy List: Army List

Naval Biog. Dictionary (Officers) (W. O'Byrne)

General Survey of Agriculture in the county of . . . Arthur Young, St John Priest and others (series of official reports by county on farmers and farming, printed c1804, some reprinted 1969–74 by David & Charles, Newton Abbot)

Returns of Owners of Land 1873 (held locally for that county only); available on microfiche for whole of England, Scotland, Wales and (1876) Ireland from MM Publications, White Cottage, Lidgate, Suffolk CB8 9PP

Dictionary of British Sculptors 1660–1851 (R. Gunnis)
Dictionary of English Architects 1660–1840 (H. M. Colvin)
Biog. Dictionary of Railway Engineers (J. Marshall)

General
Directories – Post Office, Kelly, Pigott, White etc
Town and county histories (details via local library)
Homes of Family Names: H. B. Guppy
Dictionary of Surnames: Origin of Surnames: H. Reaney
Surnames of Scotland: G. F. Black
Irish Families: E. MacLysaght

Background
Condition of the Working Class in England: Friedrich Engels (London, Manchester & Sheffield, 1844)
Rural Rides: Political Register: William Cobbett
Village Labourer: Town Labourer: J. L. & Barbara Hammond
A Woman's Work is never Done: History of Housework 1650–1950: Caroline Davidson.
Town Records: John West (data about Boroughs from earliest times.)
Local Historian's Encyclopedia: J. Richardson

INDEX